A Life Is More Than a Moment

School integration protesters marching toward Central High in August 1959. Few photographs made during the crisis have bothered me over the years as much as this picture. Every time I see the image, I wonder what effect this racist demonstration had on these innocent young men.

𝒜 Life Is More Than a Moment
The Desegregation of Little Rock's Central High

Text and Photographs by **Will Counts**
with Essays by **Will Campbell**, **Ernest Dumas**,
and **Robert S. McCord**

This book is a publication of

Indiana University Press
601 North Morton Street
Bloomington, IN 47404-3797 USA

http://www.indiana.edu/~iupress

Telephone orders 800-842-6796
Fax orders 812-855-7931
Orders by e-mail iuporder@indiana.edu

Manufactured in China

Cataloging information for this book is available from the Library of Congress.

ISBN 0-253-33637-6 (cloth)

2 3 4 5   04 03 02 01 00

School integration protesters marching toward Central High in August 1959. Few photographs made during the crisis have bothered me over the years as much as this picture. Every time I see the image, I wonder what effect this racist demonstration had on these innocent young men.

A Life Is More Than a Moment
The Desegregation of Little Rock's Central High

Text and Photographs by **Will Counts**
with Essays by **Will Campbell, Ernest Dumas,**
and **Robert S. McCord**

This book is a publication of

Indiana University Press
601 North Morton Street
Bloomington, IN 47404-3797 USA

http://www.indiana.edu/~iupress

Telephone orders 800-842-6796
Fax orders 812-855-7931
Orders by e-mail iuporder@indiana.edu

The paper used in this publication meets the minimum requrements of American National Standard for Information Sciences—Permanence of Paper for Printed Library Materials, ANSI Z39.48-1984.

Manufactured in China

Cataloging information for this book is available from the Library of Congress.

ISBN 0-253-33637-6 (cloth)

2 3 4 5   04 03 02 01 00

Dedication
To my wife, Vivian, and her new friends

Central High cheerleaders perform a routine at a pep rally before a basketball game with rival North Little Rock High School in 1999.

Contents

Like a chameleon, a photojournalist should be able to fit in, appearing to belong at the scene shooting photographs, whatever the assignment. *Photograph of Will Counts by Bob Trout.*

Preface

I HAVE OFTEN BEEN CALLED, but have never liked the word, "shutterbug." But it was probably the best moniker to describe me as a Little Rock high school student.

Before the eleventh grade, I had neither a camera nor any interest in photography. I did have a trumpet. I wanted to play the horn like Harry James and have a wife like actress Betty Grable. However, lack of musical talent and lack of enthusiasm for practice were considerable roadblocks to this career aspiration. One day in the high school library, as I was daydreaming and looking through a *Boy's Life* magazine, an ad for Speed Graphic cameras caught my attention—and strangely, from that moment on I set myself on the path to a photography career. I asked Mother for the large, expensive Speed Graphic as a Christmas present. With my father away fighting in World War II, she could only afford a Kodak Brownie Hawkeye, and with it the "shutterbug" bit deep.

It was in Miss Edna Middlebrook's eleventh-grade journalism class that I was encouraged to take photography and journalism seriously. Miss Middlebrook helped me discover that reporting the news, with words or pictures, can be a noble endeavor. The discipline and dedication she pounded into her students prepared me well for work with hard-nosed editors through the years.

Governor Orval Faubus' surprise decision in 1957 to surround Central High with Arkansas National Guard troops to prevent black students from entering aroused conflicting emotions in me. First, I was distressed that my high school was to be the focus of segregationists' efforts to stop desegregation of public schools. But also, having dreamed, studied, and prepared myself to be a photojournalist, when the troops were deployed I became very excited at the prospect of covering a major civil rights story. While covering the clashes between police and the segregation-resisting mob at Central High, I sure didn't want to look like an "Eastern Establishment" journalist. So I wore the new plaid sports shirt at the bottom of my shirt drawer. The shirt, a Christmas gift from a relative, had never been worn, but it seemed appropriate to help me blend into the mob. The shirt worked. Three *Life* magazine staffers, Francis Miller, Grey Villette, and Paul Welch, were attacked by the mob and arrested by the city police. They were dressed in coats and ties. My safety was never threatened while I was covering the violence at Central High. I was dressed like someone from the rural South—which,

I suppose, is really what I am. I grew up in small Arkansas towns: Rose Bud, Cabot, and Plum Bayou.

And it *was* exhilarating to make a contribution as the nation and the world learned of the injustices that the black students were experiencing as slowly, ever so slowly, the school began to be desegregated.

I am not a historian, but I was fortunate enough to play a part in one of the most important episodes in our country's history. This book is primarily about what I saw and photographed during Central High's crisis years of the late 1950s, as well as what I found has changed at the school in the past forty years. I have lived outside Arkansas since leaving the *Arkansas Democrat* staff in 1960 and have followed the story from a distance. Because of this, I have asked two old friends from Arkansas, Robert S. McCord and Ernest Dumas, and my new friend from Tennessee, Will Campbell, to give their insight on what has happened at Central High.

Ernest Dumas writes about how Central High has progressed since 1957. He came to Little Rock in 1961 as a reporter for the *Arkansas Gazette.* For many years he covered state government. When the *Gazette* ceased publication in 1989, Dumas became a journalism professor at the University of Central Arkansas in Conway. He continues to live in Little Rock, where his wife, Elaine, is librarian at Central High School.

Robert S. McCord was my editor at the *Arkansas Democrat* in 1957. He is the best editor I've ever worked with. He has been publishing and editing Arkansas newspapers for more than forty years. McCord and Dumas now write weekly political columns for the *Arkansas Times.*

Will Campbell was a minister who came to Little Rock when the Central High crisis began, on assignment from the National Council of Churches. He was one of several ministers who walked with the black students when they first attempted to enter Central High.

In 1957, hiding behind my camera, I admired the courage and grace exhibited by the nine black students, often called the "Little Rock Nine," who desegregated Central High. Working on this book, forty years later, I have learned to appreciate them, and what they have accomplished, much more. Getting to know Elizabeth Eckford, the only one of the nine who has continued to live in Arkansas, has been a very special joy. When she and Hazel Massery agreed to meet again at Central High, it was one of the best moments of my life.

Elizabeth's friend Annie Abrams was of great assistance in helping me learn how desegregation at Central High evolved.

Principal Rudolph Howard and his fine staff, Elaine Dumas and Assistant Principal Nancy Rousseau, kept me informed of what was going on around the school, made shooting appointments for me, and generally made my work enjoyable. I felt welcome wherever I wished to photograph. I always asked permission before shooting, but I don't recall anyone saying that they did not want to be photographed. I wish there had been room for all the photographs.

Laura Miller, Director of the Central High Museum and Visitors Center, served as my eyes in Little Rock, informing me of upcoming events and helping me make contacts. Skip Rutherford of the Cranford, Johnson, Robinson, and Woods agency made my photographs of President Clinton's visit possible.

Colleagues at my home newspaper, the *Arkansas Democrat Gazette,* welcomed me back and gave me free rein to use their newsroom and darkrooms. I particularly wish to thank Jack Schnedler and Barry Arthur, who spent much time working with me.

And, my heartfelt thanks to my dear wife, Vivian. Over the years we have grown to share so many passions, including, now, the continuing desegregation of Little Rock Central High School.

Some Little Rock churches organized demonstrations for Governor Faubus.

Ever-present pipe in mouth, Will Campbell listens on September 4, 1957, as Lt. Col. Marion Johnson, commander of the Arkansas National Guard troops at Central High, tells students Carlotta Walls, Gloria Ray, Ernest Green, and Jane Hill (in back) that his troops are under orders from Governor Orval Faubus not to allow the desegregation of Central High to begin. Campbell was one of several ministers, both black and white, who escorted the students to school. Only two weeks earlier, he had been under Lt. Col. Johnson's command at a summer National Guard camp.

Introduction
by Will Campbell

NINE LITTLE ROCK CHILDREN walking to school on a September day in 1957. Generally such scenes are like a Norman Rockwell painting. They take place in villages, small towns, and cities all over America. There is nothing unusual about it. Children in groups walking to school. It's the end of summer. Lazy days, swimming, camping, visiting grandparents, sleeping till noon: all fading memories. Time for friendly reunions, new books, new teachers, football. Happy days are here again.

There was, however, something unusual about this group walking to school. This walk, this school opening, was not of Norman Rockwell's palette. His were portraits of serenity: mother, home, and apple pie. This scene was one of meanness: rank incivility; a late summer storm. The children walking were black. A swarm of angry white people awaited them as they approached the school. There were armed soldiers to say them nay at the schoolhouse door—and a governor callously observing it all.

Melba Patillo, Ernest Green, Gloria Ray, Carlotta Walls, Terrence Roberts, Jefferson Thomas, Minnijean Brown, Thel-ma Mothershed, Elizabeth Eckford. Authentic heroes are frequently forgotten. So it is well to speak their names often and with awe. The Little Rock Nine—that would be their designation. For more than forty years they have served as a model of courage.

One of the nine, a deceptively frail-looking fifteen-year-old, had misunderstood the time they were to begin their walk of history and would face the troops and noisome throng alone. Elizabeth Eckford was her name. It was she whose abuse and humiliation would define the day.

She had slept little the night before. Such was her enthusiasm for being admitted to one of the top public high schools in the nation. She wanted to become a lawyer. She had made her dress with her own hands and pressed it carefully that morning so that she would look pretty on her first day at Central High School. And pretty she was. When she arrived alone, she saw the troops and thought they were there to protect her. Instead they blocked her entrance. In place of the friendly faces of a Rockwell painting there was an angry mob. As the soldiers turned her away, the mob moved in to carry out their mischief.

With taunts and physical threats, they followed the defenseless child as she sought a viable route of escape. Crossing the street, she started to enter a drugstore to telephone for a cab. The door was closed abruptly just as she arrived. She had not been afraid at first, thinking the soldiers were on her side. Now, as her every move was covered by the screaming mob, her composure turned to undiluted fright.

In the mob was an especially clamorous female student, with the voice and physical attributes of a cheerleader. Hazel Bryan was her name. "Nigger! Nigger! Nigger!" she screamed with animal-like frenzy. The two young women had never met. Someday they would.

Elizabeth remembers seeing a bench at a bus stop and for some reason thinking that it would offer her protection. As she moved along cautiously, slowly, the jeers became more caustic and the threats more direct. When she finally reached the bench and sat down, as if surrendering at the end of a threatening chase, she had never been more alone.

There was also a young man with a camera. Everywhere at once, trying to be inconspicuous in the teeming mass of leaderless motion but missing nothing.

Ira Wilmer Counts, Jr.

His camera was a veritable X-ray machine, probing the depths of the drama, documenting for all time precisely how the diseased organisms—the mobs, the angry taunts, rioting in the streets, political machinations—were eating away at the corpus.

In this extraordinary book of photographs you will see the most base behavior of men and women generally regarded as pillars of society—white people. You will see, to our shame, exuberant young children pouring from the segregated "Christian" academy housed in Second Baptist Church while Chris-

The education building of Little Rock's Second Baptist Church in 1958. The church opened this racially segregated private high school after Governor Orval Faubus closed the city's public high schools to avoid racial desegregation.

tian children of a darker hue are denied entrance to a school maintained by their parents' labors. Weep! We Christians.

See an interracial scene where there is charismatic dancing at a Pentecostal tent revival. Exult!

Look long and with gratitude at a short, thin man who defied the mob by sitting beside the terrified Elizabeth as the crowd closed in, lifting her head, wiping her tears, and whispering, "Don't let them see you cry." His home was New York City, his religion was Jewish. By profession he was a journalist, but with an infinite sense of decency he risked the story, put his pad aside, and may have saved the life of a helpless child; for the talk was of tree limbs and grass ropes when she sat down. Benjamin Fine.

There is also Grace Lorch. As the journalist-turned-deliverer was comforting Elizabeth, Mrs. Lorch shamed the mob into turning back. For that act of heroism she was accused by Governor Faubus of being a communist. Perhaps because he could not imagine any loyal daughter of democratic freedom doing such a thing.

"Where," the photographs cry out, "are the white Christians in this scene?"

And, of course, the beautiful and indomitable Daisy Bates. Not since "And ain't I a woman!" of Sojourner Truth fame had there been such a woman. It was Mrs. Bates, as head of the state NAACP, who sponsored, nurtured, advocated, and suffered with the children through it all.

Consider the physical beating inflicted upon Alex Wilson, a black journalist who defied the mob's orders to "Run, nigger, run!" with "I fought for my country, and I'm not going to run from you." It was a photograph that changed the course of history. When President Eisenhower saw Will Counts' pictures of Alex Wilson being beaten, with not a single advocate, he reportedly said, "I've got to do something." Two days later, the 101st Airborne Division was escorting the children to school.

Turn the pages to find the handsome, regal General Edwin Walker. His commander-in-chief ordered him to restore order and protect the children. Despite his personal feelings about black and white children attending school together, he obeyed the president's order in exacting fashion, as befitting his profession. Five years later it was this same general, now retired, who fomented a riot at the University of Mississippi to impede the integration of that institution.

Why race? Race is a sociological concept that in reality does

General Edwin Walker in front of Central High

not exist. So why keep bringing up the subject? Why is this collection of photographs, which depict so graphically something most of us would just as soon forget, so important?

Because we *must* see them. We must see them because race is an aneurysm on the heart and soul of America, a dangerous swelling on the aorta of a nation. From the landing on a continent that was the dwelling place of dark-skinned people; to the importation of black people to build what we presumptuously called the New Country; to the concocted notion of manifest destiny and our own brand of ethnic cleansing we so glibly condemn in others; to the thievery at Doak's Stand and Dancing Rabbit Creek, which led to the ignoble Trail of Tears—through it all, the aneurysm has plagued us. Occasionally the blood-filled pocket ruptures, leaving the body politic in grievous disarray. It is of such a rupturing that Will Counts' photographs speak.

It happened in Little Rock in the early fall of 1957. It might have happened anywhere in America, so the Little Rock that Mr. Counts exhibits speaks of us all. In viewing this pictorial account, we should remember that Little Rock was one of the last places in the South where it should have happened. But it did happen there, and when it did, that city became a metaphor for all the subsequent desegregation happenings in the South. It became an adjective, at times an expletive or a verb. "George Wallace Little Rocked the University of Alabama." "Ole Miss was about as Little Rocked as Governor Barnett could make it."

Many thought it would not have happened in their city except for their state's governor. And for certain, the enigmatic Orval Faubus was the catalyst who unleashed the maelstrom with which the citizens of Little Rock had to deal. You will see him here, in many poses. Faubus had been reared in an egalitarian family, his father a Norman Thomas Socialist. His reputation as governor had been one of moderation. But when he saw his political career in an impending free fall, he chose the cowardly route of exploiting a situation already filled with emotional intensity. He sent his troops to stop nine Negro children from entering Little Rock's prestigious Central High School. The Negrophobia that had simmered just under the surface in Little Rock since the lengthy federal occupation of the city following the Civil War boiled over. It spread to many parts of the South and the nation, and it did win elections. In the end, however, Faubus would die an impoverished, pathetic old man, with few to mark and mourn his passing ("How are the mighty fallen"). But in the while, he would reign as one of the nation's most popular citizens. This book is a reminder of the evil one person can perpetrate—and of how righteousness can prevail in the uncompromising resolve of a good woman and nine young warriors.

An aneurysm is always fatal when it is left unaddressed. The only antidote is major surgery. Band-aids won't do. There has never been major surgery on America's racial disunion. Will Counts, with his eye for reality, shows what happens when it is left unattended.

For the most part, Little Rock had been a peaceful city, nestling graciously in the bosom of the Arkansas River as it meandered to the Mighty Mississippi more than a hundred miles away, flowing finally into the sea, merging with the waters of many nations.

Following the organized riots and individual acts of incivility, many were surprised that it could have happened here. In Little Rock? *Time* magazine described the city as "a place of well tended homes and green lawns where violets and jonquils bloom in the spring, and chrysanthemums in autumn" (*Time*, Oct. 7, 1957). *Time* was describing the outside of the cup correctly. But they might have remembered some words of Jesus, who, in describing a similar culture, compared it to a whitewashed tomb, beautiful on the outside but inside full of dead men's bones and all sorts of iniquity. Little Rock in the spring and autumn of 1957 was indeed a city of violets and chrysanthemums. But there was also the aneurysm, the inherent racism that had never been tended, waiting now to burst.

and poison the whole body, wilting the violets of spring, stunting the mums of autumn.

There were good and honorable people in Little Rock. But for too long they had looked to the band-aids to control and contain the pout on the aorta that feeds the whole body of human relations, instead of the genuine acknowledgment and repentance of lethal racism. Some who cherished the city most saw her as a paschal lamb, sacrificed on the altar of political chicanery. Others came to see her as a city of shame. The lens of Will Counts rendered no judgment. What you see on these pages is what happened. No masquerade, no poses, no rehearsals.

As surely as Will Counts shows how one man can perpetrate a great evil, he also shows the peace that can come when an errant atones. In one of the most poignant scenes in this book, there is an important reminder: that an aneurysm of the soul need not be fatal; that genuine repentance on the part of the offending party brings sweet reconciliation. Two pictures tell the story well. Two women, in their middle years, stand side by side. In the background is the imposing and immense Little Rock Central High School, standing stately against the years, dignity and pride restored, wasted by years forgotten. We have seen these two women here before. This time the beauty of the God-made deep black skin of the one seems to enhance the same-made and equally beautiful ice-white skin of the other. Forty years earlier, it was a sad and appalling display of America at its worst. The venom dripping from the lips of the otherwise winsome Hazel Bryan added shame to shame. The sad resolve in the eyes of Elizabeth Eckford was overwhelming. In Hazel's face there was anger gone wild. Her picture had gone around the world, with only a few knowing her identity. She had long since repented of her youthful yet

Central High is still framed through the old Magnolia service station across Park Street. In 1957 the station was a gathering place for news media and others during the desegregation crisis. Now it has a new life as home of the Central High Visitors Center.

hateful misdoing, and at the same time had somehow remained the daughter of the parents who had taken her to Central High School to do precisely what she did. She had grown weary of being the "poster child of the hate generation," as she called herself. "My life has been more than that one moment."

Now here they are again—Elizabeth Eckford and Hazel

Bryan, now Hazel Bryan Massery. In the first frame they are gazing pensively away from the school. As if trying to forget. As if the one is thinking, "Where did I get that strength of courage?" The other, "Whence came that demonic monster?" And, "Whence came deliverance?"

In the second photograph they are smiling happily, laughing, really. Laughing as dear friends do, a promising refrain of "We Shall Overcome." Over the years, the Hazel pictured in 1957 had remained the anonymous screamer with a heart filled with inbred hate. She had called Elizabeth years after they, as children, drank from the bitter spring that flowed from the little rock on the banks of the Arkansas River, to beg for pardon. It was not a spontaneous triumph. There was still the scar. But it was a beginning. Healing began. Will Counts, who returned for the forty-year anniversary of the infamy of Little Rock Central High School, got the two together for these incredible photographs of them as pals. In them he shows us a glimpse of the Promised Land. It is not the Land itself but a show-and-tell of what can be. This is bonafide redemption—reconciliation, the stuff of Scripture. It leaves the viewer of this remarkable portrait of history with the feeling that the struggle has not been in vain. Something grew from that painful walk of the Little Rock Nine, that grown-up bravery of children.

They have turned out all right. One is a college professor in California. One was assistant secretary of Housing and Urban Affairs and is now managing partner of Lehmen Brothers in Washington, D.C. Another is a realtor in Colorado. Two writers, an accountant, a consultant. One lives in Canada. One is retired and lives with her husband in Sweden.

President Clinton, a fellow Arkansan, signed a bill awarding them the Congressional Gold Medal. Among children of the fifties, they have more than held their own.

These photographs have little need of commentary. Our words can be nothing more than individual expressions of our visceral response to them. In no way do they fortify the images themselves. So what, finally, is there to say? I can but share my own emotions as I view what Will Counts submits here. Thus the following:

The sin of pride is a deadly one. I suppose we are all guilty of it at times. I will not deny that for these four decades I have been pleased that I, as a young Baptist preacher from Mississippi, was one of those who walked through the mob with the Negro children to Central High School. That, however, was largely an impromptu, private, and anonymous act. Lest pride conquer discernment, there is also something which has brought neither pride nor gratification. I have wondered about it over the years. If I had been near that bench where the fifteen-year-old Elizabeth Eckford sat as the mob closed in talking of tree limbs and grass ropes, would I have had the courage of the Jewish journalist from New York and the Little Rock woman said to have been a communist? Or would I have turned away? I haven't known. Will Counts' photographs set me to wondering anew. But no matter now.

What I do know for certain is that the aneurysm on the nation's soul remains. In *A Life Is More Than a Moment,* Will Counts gives us hope.

He also sounds a warning.

A Life Is More Than a Moment

Ernest Green waited for graduation ceremonies to begin at Central High's football stadium in May 1958. Green was the only senior among the Little Rock Nine, becoming the first black student to graduate from the school.

A Perspective of Central High
by Ernest Dumas

BEFORE IT BECAME a symbol for bigotry and the South's resistance to integration, Little Rock Central High School had a reputation of another sort, as the premier high school in Arkansas, the place where ambitious parents outside the school district finagled to get their youngsters enrolled. But in a state where education traditionally had trifling value, being recognized as the best school may amount to small praise. Indeed, fewer of Arkansas's children went to high school, or graduated, or went on to college than did those in any other state. In 1930, three years after Central High was built, only 8 percent of the youngsters of high school age in Arkansas attended school, and a popular conservative who was elected governor two years later tried to end funding altogether for high schools in the state, on the grounds that any education beyond elementary school was superfluous for most children and a scandalous waste of money for a poor state. Educational achievement was not a high public value, and neither did a great many families covet it for their children. Arkansas ranked dead last among the states in about every way you could measure either effort or achievement in education.

After World War II, public education made considerable strides throughout the state—a quality education for every child was at least the official doctrine—but at the time Governor Orval Faubus made it a national battleground over school integration in 1957, Central High still stood out as an academic oasis. Wherever there was a competition—bands, newspapers, writing, science, athletic teams—Central's students nearly always dominated.

When Central opened in September 1927 as Little Rock Senior High School, the *New York Times* said it was the most expensive schoolhouse ever constructed in the United States. It cost $1.5 million. The building was massive—it measured 564 by 365 feet and housed 100 classrooms with a capacity of 3,000 students. The American Institute of Architects selected it as "the Most Beautiful High School in America." Its most prominent feature, which would become familiar to the world in 1957–59, was a phalanx of statues of classical figures above the front portals personifying Ambition, Opportunity, Preparation, and Personality. The school opened with just under 1,800 high school and junior college students.

Though the building was not quite so large and impressive, the city two years later opened another fine high school, this one for African-Americans, only a few blocks to the east. At Dunbar High School, the city did not spend the money it dedicated to the expansive programs at Central, but few schools for African-Americans below the Mason-Dixon line matched it. It became the first African-American high school in Arkansas to be accredited by the North Central Association for Colleges and Schools. Elsewhere across Arkansas, high schools for blacks were either nonexistent, far away, or likely to be so inferior that graduating from them was hardly worthwhile, Dunbar routinely enrolled African-American children from the surrounding school districts, and families from across the state often sent their children to live with relatives in Little Rock so they could attend Dunbar. The variety and quality of the programs at Central High were so superior to those offered in the surrounding districts that white parents in those communities often made tuition arrangements or accommodations with relatives and friends at Little Rock to have their children enrolled at Central.

The school's reputation spread beyond the state. In 1957, a survey rated it one of the top thirty-eight high schools in the United States, on the basis of the scholarship performance of its graduates and the scores of seniors on National Merit examinations. Of the seniors who graduated in the spring of the confrontation, sixty-two won college scholarships and nineteen were National Merit semifinalists—13 percent of all those selected in Arkansas. Another seven Central students who qualified as National Merit semifinalists were transferred to the new Hall High School for their senior year. (National Merit semifinalists are those in each state who score in the top one-half of one percent on a portion of the Scholastic Aptitude Test.)

If Central High School was the least likely spot in the South for the forces of intolerance and fear to take their stand against the tide of social change loosed by the Supreme Court's order to desegregate the schools, Little Rock was about the least likely host for the confrontation. It was no redneck capital. At least as far back as the 1920s, adults in Little Rock had exceeded those in the nation as a whole in the levels of completed education and, of course, far exceeded the education levels of the rest of Arkansas. Though its schools, like those everywhere in the South, remained segregated, by the mid-1950s Little Rock at least was trying to approach the legal standard of "separate

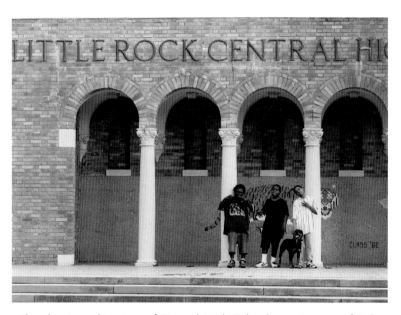

The classic architecture of Central High School remains one of Little Rock's most impressive tourist attractions. These boys playing around the school's mosaic tiger lived in the neighborhood, which is now often described as "Inner City." I was told later by a Central High student that the kids were flashing gang signs as they postured for my camera.

Even during the heat of the desegregation crisis, there was always evidence of individual personal friendships between blacks and whites in Little Rock. These women were chatting on a street near Central High School.

but equal," the doctrine used by the Supreme Court in 1897 to justify legal segregation. Nearly everywhere in the South, "separate but equal" was honored in law but not in practice. In 1952, per-pupil spending in African-American schools in Little Rock reached 93 percent of the spending level in the white schools, and by 1954 every African-American school in the city had received the highest accreditation by the Arkansas Department of Education. Five days after the Supreme Court declared segregated schools unconstitutional in May 1954, the Little Rock School Board declared that it would end its dual school system. A year later, the school board adopted a plan to desegregate the city's schools in stages, starting with Central High School in 1957. The community seemed to take it in stride.

Left to their own devices, the students and faculty at Central High would have carried out the first integration of education with the school's usual aplomb. When the governor, yielding to political fear, sent the state militia to turn back the nine black children who were to attend the school in September 1957, students and teachers entered the building each day through hecklers, mobs, soldiers, and reporters. Eventually, President Eisenhower changed the mission of the soldiers from defiance to protection of the black students, which calmed the commotion outside. Inside, classes and activities went on as usual, marred by occasional racial epithets, shoves, and trippings. The African-American students would remember the ugly shibboleths and sneers, the occasional expressions of support and graciousness, and what seemed like indifference on the part of a vast majority of the students. White students would recall a more normal year, most of them not having witnessed but only heard about the verbal and physical incidents. They were much more likely to remember the undefeated football team, which extended its string of successive

Segregated elementary and junior high schools remained in session during the desegregation crisis at Central High School. These black elementary school students had to walk through the crowd of protesters and newspersons camped out around Central High.

victories to thirty-three, including wins over the top-ranked teams in Louisiana, Kentucky, and Texas.

Order returned to Central High School, but tranquillity was harder to restore. The school's reputation, like the city's and Arkansas's, had been sullied, though by forces and events beyond its control. Living down the stigma of bigotry and lawlessness is not the perfect motivation for an educational program, but tradition provides a powerful incentive. It helped that the faculty and administrators at Central had known a much higher estimation.

A defiled reputation was not the school's only obstacle. Central was located in the old heart of a city that was expanding westward along the Arkansas River into the foothills of the Ozarks. Coincident with the integration of Central High, the school board had built a new high school to serve the children of the gorgeous subdivisions that were materializing in the wooded outcroppings in the western reaches of town. Fifteen years later, it would build still another on the western perimeter. People in the old inner city could be forgiven a little class consciousness. The old working-class neighborhoods would bear the stresses of the social experiment of school integration, while the affluent white preserves would enjoy pristine white schools that would be spared the strains of educating children of both races in the same classrooms. Central did carry the brunt of integration at the secondary level for a few years under the district's "freedom of choice" pupil-assignment plan, but integration proved to be token citywide, as it did in other Southern cities that followed the freedom-of-choice plans. A dozen years after the Central High crisis, the city had to prepare a plan to bring about a reasonable racial balance in all its schools, and cross-city busing began on a large scale. In 1971, the school board proposed to the federal court that Central High become a junior high school to facilitate a racial balance in the junior and senior high schools. Students, teachers, and parents protested, and the federal court rejected the plan. Owing to the uncertainty about its future, Central's enrollment sank from 2,000 to fewer than 1,500.

Uncertainty and turmoil—and, especially, busing—drove thousands from the city's public schools. Private academies opened and flourished all over the county, and families fled to the suburbs ringing the city or to cities in adjoining counties, leaving the Little Rock schools—and, to a slightly lesser extent, the city itself—with a higher and higher percentage of blacks. African-Americans accounted for 23 percent of the city's population in 1960 and 35 percent in 1990, but because of the changing demographics of the racial groups, the racial ratio of school-aged children in 1990 had reached fifty-fifty. Owing to the flourishing private schools in and around the city, however, the ratio in the school population had reached fifty-fifty sixteen years earlier, in 1974. By 1997, 67 percent of the children in the city's public schools were African-American, and about 40 percent of all the white children in the city were enrolled in private or parochial schools. To attract and retain white students, the city in the 1980s turned the high schools on the west side into magnets and specialty schools.

The migratory population was having another effect on Central High. In the 1950s, the school had been the hub of an aging but stable middle-class community. The neighborhood was predominantly white, but the races lived in close proximity. A quarter-century later, the area was predominantly poor and black and suffered from one of the highest violent crime rates in the state. Crumbling and vacant buildings surrounded the school, and crack houses saturated the neighborhood. The violence occasionally spilled over into the halls and offices of Central High. Warring gangs carried their vendettas onto the campus, and sullen, adventurous, or crazed young men could find their way into the hallways through one of the cavernous school's many entrances. A violent disturbance at Central High was certain to make the front pages of the state's newspapers and lead the television news.

How an educational institution vulnerable to parental alarm withstood such vicissitudes, attracted bright children, and maintained a standard of excellence became something of a mystery. Morris Holmes, Central's second African-American principal, who was credited with the school's renaissance in the mid- to late 1970s, said it was because of "one great faculty in terms of intellect, training, scholarship and dedication—that's what this school rides on right now." Roosevelt Thompson, the son of a black preacher, became the personification of the school. Thompson was an all-state football player for the Central Tigers in the late 1970s, was president of the student body in 1980, starred in the senior play, earned the highest

score in the state on the National Merit examination, and maintained a perfect 4.0 average through high school. He was an honor student, an athlete, and residential college president at Yale University. "There were some shaky years at Central when it could have gone either way, but the consciousness of 1957, the community, and all the factors inside the school have made it work," Thompson said in a newspaper interview in 1982. Shortly afterward, Thompson, who had been chosen a Rhodes Scholar, was killed in a car accident on the New Jersey Turnpike.

Despite massive white flight from the inner city, crime-ridden surroundings, and the lure of rich programs at magnet schools, Central High on the fortieth anniversary of the crisis burnished its reputation as the pre-eminent high school in the region. The school offers four foreign languages (formerly six) and more than one hundred courses, including thirteen ad-

Some of the 1997 Central students who were accepted to out-of-state universities pose with their guidance counselor, Sam Blair. Front row: Larissa Jennings (Harvard), Salima Shaikh (Wellesley), Sarah Keith (Brown), Jett McAlister (Rice), Ryan Davis (Lake Forest), and Martha Brantley (Yale). Back row: David Slade (Yale), Jenny Holt (Indiana University), Salonica Gray (Vanderbilt), and Adam Light (University of Chicago.)

The exterior of Central High has something of the appearance of a fortress, and even the hallways have a strong institutional feel, but the students have a friendly spontaneity that makes the building seem warm. In 1997 these students from Lois Thompson's tenth grade literature class were practicing a presentation on Shakespeare's *A Midsummer Night's Dream* outside their third-floor classroom.

vanced-placement courses. Here are a few manifestations of its excellence: In 1997, twenty-three Central seniors were chosen National Merit semifinalists, a sixth of all the semifinalists in Arkansas. Until the opening of a state mathematics and science high school in 1991, the school had more National Merit semifinalists every year than any other school in the state. Five percent or more of its graduating seniors regularly are accepted at Ivy League or other very selective liberal arts colleges and universities. Members of the 1997 graduating class were accepted at seven of the eight Ivy League schools, including three at Harvard and two at Yale. Ninety-seven of its graduates accepted 128 scholarships valued at $1,801,000. Central students nearly every year win one or two of Arkansas's six National Council of Teachers of English writing awards. The

school has produced nearly as many winners of National Achievement Scholarships, reserved for high-achieving African-American students, as the rest of the state combined, and in the 1990s it produced half of the African-American students in Arkansas who qualified as National Merit semifinalists. *College Bound*, a professional journal published by the College Board, reported in 1994 that Central High was among twenty-six public high schools most often identified by the admissions deans of the country's most selective colleges and universities as schools that best prepare students, year in and year out, for highly selective universities. Forty years after the ignominy of 1957, the old school had parted from her disgrace and restored the eminence of her youth.

Officers of the 101st Airborne Division, led by General Edwin Walker, inspect the troop deployment at Central High in September 1957.

An Unexpected Crisis
by Robert S. McCord

*A*s USUAL, Labor Day in 1957 in Little Rock was muggy and hot, with temperatures in the 90s. After the picnics, boat rides, and holiday trips had ended, most people turned on the television before going to bed—and to their surprise, there was Governor Orval Faubus announcing that he had just called out the National Guard to prevent nine black children from enrolling at Central High School the next morning.

Because Little Rock's decision to integrate had been voluntary and without much controversy, some people couldn't believe what they heard. So at 11 P.M. they got in their cars and cruised slowly around Central High School, Little Rock's symbol of intellectualism. They saw three hundred armed soldiers already in place, guarding every door.

In his TV speech, Faubus said that he had called out the Guard to prevent violence, which he said was his obligation as governor, a claim he maintained until he died in 1994. But since a federal court only two days before had declared that no one should interfere with the planned integration of Central High School, Faubus' action made him the first governor in the United States in modern times to try to impose his power over the federal government.

Arkansas is not the Deep South. It took two votes, months apart, and the actual beginning of the Civil War before delegates agreed to take Arkansas into the Confederacy. Unlike other Southern states, Arkansas never passed laws that prohibited blacks from being educated, although they had to attend their own schools rather than go to school with whites.

Arkansas blacks never even pushed hard for their rights until World War II. According to John A. Kirk, a historian writing in the *Arkansas Historical Quarterly*, the guiding philosophy for blacks in Arkansas was Booker T. Washington's "accommodation," which meant economic advancement within the boundaries of segregation. There were exceptions, of course, but before the 1940s the relatively successful black businessmen in Little Rock were so comfortable that the National Association for the Advancement of Colored People got virtually no support in the state.

That changed, according to Kirk, after a Pine Bluff lawyer, Harold Flowers, founded what he called the Committee on

One-time moderate Governor Orval Faubus waited to start a televised address from the Arkansas governor's mansion.

While much of it was tokenism, racial progress began arriving in Arkansas more quickly than in most Southern states. In the 1940s, newspapers in Little Rock began publishing stories and pictures of blacks that pertained to things other than crime, and one of the newspapers, the *Arkansas Democrat,* hired a black reporter. In 1948, the University of Arkansas at Fayetteville became the first law school in the South to admit a black. The medical school accepted a black female student the same year. The public library in Little Rock was quietly desegregated, some "White Only" signs came down, and blacks for the first time were quietly admitted to public parks and the Little Rock Zoo. Three days after the Supreme Court banned discrimination on intrastate buses in 1956, Little Rock integrated its bus service with no difficulty. Republican and Democratic state committees in Arkansas had black members before those in any other Southern state, and Arkansas repealed the poll tax (a device that kept poor blacks from voting) a year before Congress made the tax illegal in 1965.

Six years before the Supreme Court's desegregation decision (*Brown vs. Board of Education*), lawyer Flowers was filing lawsuits asking for equal facilities for blacks in four Arkansas cities. Seven cities with very few black residents voluntarily integrated their schools, including Charleston, which on August 23, 1954, became the first city in the eleven Confederate states to desegregate its schools.

Charleston, of course, was a tiny community with so few black families that it never built any black schools. It was a financial saving for Charleston to be able to stop busing a handful of black children every day to black schools in a nearby, larger city. There were lots of situations like that in the state; the bulk of the black population was in eastern and southern Arkansas, in the agricultural areas. In 1957, Arkansas had 1.7 million people, and about 22 percent of them were black—a

Negro Organizations. Blacks began to push for their rights and to vote. In 1942, a black Little Rock school teacher went to federal court to demand that she be paid the same salary as white teachers, the first successful attempt by a black Arkansan to win equal rights in the courts. The NAACP's Thurgood Marshall made his first trip to Arkansas to win this case.

L. C. and Daisy Bates started their black newspaper, the *State Press,* and its editorials about the killing of a black soldier by a white policeman led to the appointment of black police officers in Little Rock. With the support of the newspaper, a black minister announced for alderman in Little Rock in 1950. Denied the right to run in the Democratic primary, he went to court and won, ending the all-white primary system in Arkansas, although losing the election.

During the summer of 1958, as Little Rock was gaining notoriety as a racist city because of the continuing crisis at Central High, I found blacks and whites worshiping together in a racially integrated revival service held in a tent on South Main Street. Whites outnumbered blacks during the service; however, that didn't deter this black woman from dancing in front of the congregation.

smaller ratio than in all but four of the eleven states in the old Confederacy. Little Rock, the state's largest city, with a population of 108,000, was 23.5 percent black.

Notwithstanding the demagoguery heard from politicians in many states after the Supreme Court decision, the governor of Arkansas, Francis Cherry, who was later defeated by Faubus, declared, "Arkansas will obey the law." And even Faubus said, "It appears that the Court left some degree of decision in these matters to the federal district courts. I believe this will guarantee against any sudden dislocation."

Of course, as Will Counts' photographs show, Faubus was wrong about that.

In 1954, Faubus, running as a populist against the incumbent Francis Cherry, a former judge, won the Democratic primary by only 6,819 votes. He had the support of the liberal community and the *Arkansas Gazette* because Cherry, in desperation, had attacked Faubus for having briefly attended a socialist college in southwest Arkansas. The *Gazette* called it McCarthyism.

But the closeness of the vote convinced Faubus that there was little political security in liberalism in the South following the Supreme Court's desegregation decision. Faubus, who was born and reared in the Arkansas hills, where there were almost no blacks, had a poll taken that showed that 85 percent of Arkansans opposed school integration. In 1956, when his opposition turned out to be Jim Johnson, an ardent segregationist politician, Faubus promised the voters that "no school district will be forced to mix the races as long as I am governor of Arkansas."

Faubus won. So did three initiated acts favoring segregation that the legislature had passed and Faubus had signed. In its 1957 session, the legislature passed four more segregation laws, including one that allowed parents to refuse to send their students to integrated schools. Supporters of segregation, including other Southern governors, pressed Faubus to join them and openly resist integration. One governor, Marvin Griffin of Georgia, came to Little Rock to talk to the rapidly growing White Citizens Council and attracted a large crowd with his anti-integration speech. He said he would call out the National Guard to prevent integration in his state.

A rock bearing a note that read "Stone this time, dynamite next" was thrown through a window of the home of Daisy and L. C. Bates, and a cross was burned in their yard. After a federal judge turned down a last-minute delay for the integration of Central High School, Faubus said he had been told that mobs from eastern Arkansas were poised to descend on Little Rock when Central opened the day after Labor Day. He had ordered a check of weapons sales in Little Rock and reported that they were increasing. The Central High Mothers League, a segregationist group, asked a state court to postpone integration, and Faubus testified in their behalf, talking about the increase in weapons sales and "caravans" of segregationists en route to Little Rock. The reports of both weapons sales and the "caravans" of troublemakers turned out to be false—the work of Jim Johnson and other segregationists, including Faubus supporters. But the circuit judge granted the delay.

Emboldened by this news, Faubus made up his mind. The governor, at one time considered a liberal, even a socialist, decided to call out the Guard. Why? "Unabashed expediency," wrote Harry Ashmore, the late editor of the *Arkansas Gazette,* who won a Pulitzer Prize for his editorials against Faubus. "I never questioned Faubus' assertion that he was not a racist." Faubus knew he had to do this if he had any chance to win a third term, Ashmore wrote in his book *Civil Rights and Wrongs.*

But it was more complicated than that, says Roy Reed, the author of *Faubus: The Life and Times of an American Prodigal.*

After the Little Rock Nine began classes at desegregated Central High under the protection of federalized National Guardsmen, very seldom did newsmen have access to them. One exception was when all nine gathered at the home of Daisy Bates, Arkansas NAACP chapter president, for Thanksgiving dinner in 1957. L. C. Bates (left) sits at the head of the table next to his wife, Daisy. Clockwise from her are Jefferson Thomas, Elizabeth Eckford, Ernest Green, Minnijean Brown, an unidentified NAACP official, Gloria Ray, Carlotta Walls, Terrence Roberts, Melba Patillo, and Thelma Mothershed.

National and local newsmen crowded around Governor Orval Faubus' desk for a press conference in his office. These general press briefings often produced little news, as the governor often talked first to *Arkansas Democrat* reporter George Douthit (back row center in the white shirt with the open collar). I don't recall Faubus ever addressing the welfare of black students, either those who were attempting to desegregate the all-white schools or those who were shut out of all the Little Rock public high schools when he closed them to avoid having blacks and whites attend school together.

Faubus was never one of those politicians who claimed the superiority of the white race, but there were plenty in the South and in Arkansas who did. Faubus was right, according to Reed, when he said that had he not resisted segregation, he would have been turned out of office and a genuine racist would have been elected.

Reed also found merit in Faubus' complaint that 85 percent of the Southern members of Congress (including every congressman and senator from Arkansas) had signed the Southern manifesto, which called the Supreme Court's decision "an abuse of judicial power" and urged the states "to resist forced integration by any means." That done, they stepped to the sidelines and let the governors take care of the problem.

"He [Faubus] acted for the same reason they did: to save his political hide," Reed wrote. "If avoiding political suicide was not admirable in Orval Faubus, it was no more so in the scores of senators and representatives who signed their names to a pandering public lie for the same reason."

The morning after Faubus' Labor Day speech, a crowd of about three hundred gathered across the street from the high school and stared at the National Guardsmen. But there was nothing for them to protest, because the black children had been told to stay home out of fear that there would be violence. That afternoon, a federal judge overruled the state court's postponement and ordered desegregation to begin the next day.

So the next morning, all but one, Elizabeth Eckford, were accompanied by black and white ministers as they attempted to enter the school. The crowd was back, and it grew angry when the black children showed up at the school's door. National Guardsmen, acting on the governor's orders, refused to allow them to enter, and they left rapidly in cars.

By now, Little Rock had become the focus of the national press, as hundreds of reporters began to arrive at the site of the first resistance to integration by a large city. Mayor Woodrow Mann accused Faubus of a "hoax" in calling out the National Guard on the pretext of violence, and Mann said there was no danger of violence that the city could not control.

However, the Little Rock City Council sided with Faubus and rebuked Mayor Mann, who later was run out of office and moved to Texas.

But by now the school board feared violence. It asked the

Governor Faubus joined with School Superintendent Virgil Blossom to answer questions from the media after the Little Rock School Board asked the federal court for a delay in starting integration. Usually Governor Faubus was chiding Superintendent Blossom and the school board because they had drafted and sponsored the desegregation plan approved by the federal court.

federal court to grant a temporary delay in the integration of the school. Thurgood Marshall came to oppose the school board's petition, and federal judge Ronald Davies denied any delay. Faubus went on television and defended his actions, hitting the ball into the federal government's court, and it responded with a summons ordering the governor and two National Guard officers to attend a hearing in federal court in ten days to decide why an injunction should not be issued to stop them from interfering with the orders of a federal court. The black students decided to await the outcome of the hearing before making another attempt to integrate Central High School.

Meanwhile, moderate Arkansas congressman Brooks Hays became the go-between for Faubus and President Eisenhower and arranged a meeting between the two men. (For his trouble, the congressman, then in his eighth term, was defeated by a write-in segregationist at the next election.) In his book, Ashmore wrote that Eisenhower, who had never before taken a public position on the Supreme Court's desegregation decision, was sympathetic to Faubus and Hays' request for a cooling-off period, but that Attorney General Herbert Brownell insisted that the matter was in the hands of the federal courts and was not one to be decided by the executive branch of government.

After a two-hour meeting, the president and the governor announced that they had reached an agreement, and each issued a statement. Faubus said that the Supreme Court's decision in *Brown vs. Board of Education* "was the law of the land and must be obeyed. The people of Little Rock are law-abiding, and I know that they expect to obey valid court orders."

The agreement lasted exactly six days. After hearing testimony and studying a 400-page FBI report on the chances of violence in Little Rock, Judge Davies on Friday, September 20, enjoined Governor Faubus and the National Guard from fur-

Judge Ronald Davies posed in his Little Rock federal court chambers. Judge Davies was temporarily assigned to Arkansas from North Dakota to handle cases relating to the desegregation of Little Rock Central High. He kept a low public profile during his few months in Arkansas.

The NAACP's chief counsel, Thurgood Marshall, holds the door for Daisy Bates, Gloria Ray, and Minnijean Brown as they exit the Little Rock Federal District courtroom. Marshall had argued the *Brown vs. Board of Education* case before the U.S. Supreme Court in 1954. Later, he was appointed the first black justice of the U.S. Supreme Court.

ther interference at Central High School. Three hours later, Faubus went on television and ordered the National Guard to withdraw, saying that he would do "everything in my power" to keep the peace at the school. The Legislative Council presented Faubus with a framed certificate of accommodation for his handling of the situation at Central High School just before Faubus left to attend a meeting of the Southern Governors Conference in Sea Island, Georgia, where he was treated like a hero.

Mayor Mann said the Little Rock police would take the place of the National Guard and preserve order at the school on Monday, when the blacks were to be admitted. The school board asked that all adults stay away from the school building—a request that was totally ignored. By 8 A.M. Monday, there were a thousand people around the school, and it was a mob, not a crowd. They turned on the first black people they saw—seven black journalists who were trying to report the event.

The black children had gathered at the Bateses' home, from which they left in cars for the high school. Police met them and escorted them through a side entrance without incident. Someone in the mob saw them, and, according to Mrs. Bates, the mob rushed toward the cars shouting, "They're in, the niggers are in!"

This inflamed the mob, which by that time, because of hysterical radio reports, had grown to several thousand people. Some began shouting to the white students who were hanging out of the windows watching the mob: "Come out! Don't stay in there with those niggers!" At least fifty left the building.

At that point, some of the protesters turned on what they called the "Yankee reporters." Two black women driving near the high school were pulled out of their car and beaten. So were two black men in a truck.

The police were seriously outnumbered, and the mob was out of control. Gene Smith, the assistant chief of police, was worried; the fire department was supposed to be on hand to halt the mob with water hoses, but the firemen refused to take part. Smith decided to withdraw the black children from the school, and he sent police cars to a secluded entrance to pick them up. When it was announced over a public address system that the students were no longer inside the school, the mob gradually calmed down and drifted off.

But Little Rock was stunned. "The citizens of Little Rock

English teacher Emily Penton talked with Elizabeth Eckford during the few hours the Little Rock Nine attended class on September 23, 1957. Because of the violence outside, the black students were escorted from the school by Little Rock policemen. This photograph was probably made by a student in Miss Penton's class. It was published and copyrighted by the *Arkansas Democrat* without a photographer's credit. Somehow it made its way into my file of Central High negatives.

U.S. 101st Airborne troops helped Carlotta Walls (left) and Minnijean Brown from a government station wagon when they arrived to begin classes on September 25, 1957.

had witnessed a savage rebirth of passion and racial hatred that had lain dormant since Reconstruction days," according to Daisy Bates in her book *The Long Shadow of Little Rock.*

But in terms of actual casualties, it wasn't so bad. There were several bad beatings. Twenty-five arrests were made at the school, and about twenty other people were taken into custody in other parts of town as gangs of black and white youths roamed the city. Harry Ashmore said, "The psychic damage was heavy. The television and still cameras sought out the naked face of hatred . . . to the point where Little Rock became the symbol of brutal, dead-end resistance to the minimum requirements of racial justice."

The next day, President Eisenhower, denouncing what he called "disgraceful occurrences," federalized the Arkansas National Guard and ordered the units back to Central High School. That night he sent in twelve hundred paratroopers from the 101st Airborne Division in Fort Campbell, Kentucky. Their trucks and jeeps created an ironic picture for photographers as they rumbled past a billboard in downtown Little Rock that read: "Who will build Arkansas if her own people will not?"

The next morning, paratroopers met the nine black students at Mrs. Bates' home and drove them to Central High School under heavy guard. About twenty-five soldiers went inside the building with the black students to protect them from being injured by disgruntled white students. A crowd of

Surrounded by federal troops from the 101st Airborne, nine black students walked up the steps to begin the desegregation of Central High School on September 25, 1957.

Minnijean Brown chatted with classmates as they clustered during a Central High bomb scare in 1957. Minnijean said in 1997 that she believes the students would have eventually accepted her as a classmate and friend. However, she was expelled for dumping chili on a white student who had been harassing her in the school cafeteria.

about a hundred gathered in front of the school, but it was quickly dispersed by the paratroopers, who had bayonets on their rifles. At least one man who refused to move when told to received bayonet cuts, and two men were clubbed with rifle butts.

Faubus returned from the Southern Governors Conference and made a speech that was televised nationally. He said that Arkansas was now "occupied territory," and that the American people would one day rebuke Eisenhower for sending federal troops to Little Rock. A reporter reminded Faubus that at the meeting with Eisenhower he had said that Supreme Court orders had to be obeyed. Faubus then replied with a quote that

journalists never allowed him to forget: "Just because I said it doesn't make it so."

The paratroopers stayed on duty until November 18, leaving the federalized Arkansas National Guard to preserve the peace. But most of the violence was inside rather than outside Central High. One of the nine, Minnijean Brown, was being harassed daily in the cafeteria, so one day she dumped a bowl of chili on two of her tormentors. Eventually Minnijean was expelled, as were many white antagonists of the black students. Gloria Ray, for example, was pushed down a flight of stairs, and there were innumerable assaults on the blacks by a small gang of white boys dedicated to that purpose. Isolated violence committed by disgruntled segregationists also continued in the community. A bomb exploded at the home of Daisy and L. C. Bates, leaving a crater in the lawn.

In February of 1958, the Little Rock School Board asked the federal court for a delay in integration beginning with the next year of school. The board wanted to revert to segregated schools until the Supreme Court defined exactly what it meant by desegregating "with all deliberate speed." By then Judge Davies, who had come temporarily to Arkansas from North Dakota to replace a retiring Arkansas district judge, had been replaced by Judge Harry Lemley, and in June the latter agreed with the school board, granting the delay. "Blacks have a

With this handshake and a pat on the back at a 1958 campaign rally, Governor Orval Faubus demonstrated that he could be "one of the good ole boys." This ability seems to be a trait of successful politicians everywhere.

constitutional right to attend white schools, but the events in Little Rock have shown that the time to exercise those rights has not come," Lemley said.

The NAACP appealed to the Eighth Circuit Court of Appeals, which reversed Judge Lemley's decision, declaring: "We say the time has not come in these United States when an order of a federal court must be whittled away, watered down or shamefully withdrawn in the face of violent acts of individual citizens."

The school board appealed to the Supreme Court, which interrupted its summer recess to give unanimous approval to the Eighth Circuit Court's decision.

Meanwhile, Faubus had won nomination for a third term, collecting 69 percent of the votes. He called a special session of the legislature to pass several anti-integration measures, including one that would allow a vote of the people to close any school. After the school board announced that blacks would be admitted to all high schools starting in September, Faubus invoked the new law, and the people of Little Rock voted 19,470 to 7,561 to close all the public high schools. Faubus wanted the school taxes to be turned over to a private high school that segregationists had opened in an abandoned University of Arkansas building, but the federal courts ruled that out. About 1,000 white students enrolled in it and a Baptist high school that was hurriedly created. The result: 3,698 other high school students, white and black, had to find schools to attend in other cities.

Segregationists clearly had the upper hand. Jim Johnson was elected to the state supreme court. A Gallup Poll named Faubus one of the ten men most admired by Americans (no other governor had ever received the honor). The Little Rock School Board resigned in frustration over the closed high schools. A new board was elected that included three avowed

This misleading sign appeared on the Central High lawn in 1958, the day after Governor Faubus announced that he had ordered the city's high schools closed to stop the federal court–ordered desegregation plan.

Students at private Raney High School, which opened in 1958 after Governor Orval Faubus closed the public high schools, rally on their small campus in support of the governor. The school, named for a close friend of the governor, was established in an old building about a block from my family home on Lewis Street. It had contained a nursing home and classrooms for University of Arkansas night classes.

Opposition to Governor Faubus' school-closing policies grew after the school board fired 44 teachers because they were suspected of working for racial integration to reopen the public high schools. The stage of Little Rock's Robinson Auditorium was filled with members of STOP (Stop This Outrageous Purge) and the Women's Emergency Committee during a Little Rock School Board recall election rally on May 19, 1959.

segregationists, and they fired forty-four teachers who had spoken up for integration or been friendly to the black students at Central High School.

Until this point, civic leaders had been unwilling to criticize publicly either Faubus or the segregationists, although they realized that the image of Little Rock and the state was being tarnished. For example, a reporter called the president of the Arkansas State Chamber of Commerce, the state's largest business organization, and asked him if he thought Faubus' actions had hurt the Arkansas economy. "I'm not going to answer," he said, "and furthermore, I don't want you even to write that you called me and asked me that question."

But the purging of the teachers broke their timidity. The Little Rock Chamber of Commerce announced that it had taken a poll, and that its members had voted four to one to

reopen the public schools on a desegregated basis. Three days after the purge, 179 businessmen and civic leaders met to form an organization to recall the three segregationist school board members. They called it STOP—Stop This Outrageous Purge. The segregationists quickly organized to support their school board members; the acronym they chose was CROSS—the Committee to Retain Our Segregated Schools.

Adolphine Terry, the wife of a former Arkansas congressman, had formed the Women's Emergency Committee to Open Our Schools, but it had had little success. However, it did have a large membership, which it rallied, enabling STOP to narrowly win the election and vote out the segregationist board members. The new board rehired thirty-nine of the forty-four teachers who had been fired.

Another victory came the very next month. A three-judge

24

From the back of a truck trailer, STOP workers checked petitions asking for a special recall election in May 1959 of three school board members who supported Governor Faubus' closing schools to avoid racial integration.

Supporters of Governor Orval Faubus' closing of Little Rock high schools to avoid racial integration rallied at MacArthur Park in May 1959. CROSS is an acronym for the Committee to Retain our Segregated Schools.

federal district court ruled that the Arkansas school-closing law was unconstitutional. The Little Rock School Board announced that the public high schools would reopen, with some black students attending both Central and Hall high schools. Anyway, by this time both of the private high schools had run out of money and had to close.

Two hundred and fifty protesters began a march on Central High School from the state capitol. When they tried to break through police lines, the firemen were there this time to turn hoses on them. Twenty-one of the protesters were arrested.

It was Little Rock's last big school-segregation rally, but the violence was not over.

Two weeks later, two women who were never identified threw tear gas into a building where the school board was meeting on the second floor. Five men—one of them the owner of a lumber company—used dynamite to blow up the fire chief's car, damage a commercial building owned by the mayor, and wreck a part of the school administration building. All the bombers were arrested, convicted, and sent to prison.

In the months and years that followed, there were many other school-integration crises around the country, several of them much more serious than Little Rock's. But there had to be a first one. The federal government had underestimated the reaction to the Supreme Court's desegregation decision, and the decision itself provided no specifics as to how or when desegregation was to take place. Some of these answers were learned in Little Rock. It was a confrontation that had to happen.

The last desegregation protest march, in August 1959, was stopped a block from Central High by Little Rock City policemen led by Chief Gene Smith (center). Soon afterwards, Smith committed suicide, reportedly because of the stress of his job in trying to maintain order in Little Rock during the explosive times of the crisis at Central High.

After hearing Governor Faubus and other pro-segregation speakers, marchers filled High Street, now Martin Luther King Jr. Blvd., on their way to Central High school in August 1959.

In earlier encounters betweeen school-segregationist protesters and Little Rock police, the city firemen had refused to allow their fire hose to be used to control the crowd. In August 1959, however, high-power water helped keep marchers from reaching Central High School.

Covering the Crisis

*J*HE LITTLE ROCK NEWS MEDIA didn't expect the beginning of integration at Central High to be that big a story. The *Arkansas Gazette*'s headline on Labor Day morning read "Little Rock Quiet on Eve of Opening Integrated Schools." That afternoon, the *Arkansas Democrat*'s one-column headline was "18,000 Expected by City Schools," with the beginning of racial integration relegated to a subhead, "15 or Less Stated to Be Integrated at High School."

It seemed obvious that when the state's chief executive placed his office in direct defiance of the U.S. Federal Court order authorizing the desegregation of Central High, a major confrontation between state and federal rights was developing. But it was only after the Guard troops were deployed at Central that the news staff of my paper, the *Arkansas Democrat,* began to gear up for extensive coverage. I had been working at the *Democrat* for only about three months. Like many native Arkansans in the 1950s, I had been out of state for study and work. I returned home primarily for the opportunity to work with Robert McCord, and the staff he had gathered for the *Democrat*'s Sunday Magazine. In this magazine position I was not normally

assigned to spot news stories, which turned out to be a big advantage in my work at Central High. The other *Democrat* photographers were under deadline pressures to shoot images quickly for the day's afternoon editions, so they stayed positioned in a pack with most of the other media. I was free to go elsewhere. Much of the action at Central High occurred away from the media pack.

As a news photographer I was preparing to record whatever happened at Central that morning of September 4th, but personally I desperately wanted the school's integration to go smoothly. I grew up believing in racial integration. In 1936, when I was five, my farming parents had the opportunity to move to Plum Bayou, a Roosevelt administration resettlement community near England, Arkansas. While this federal project followed the state's segregation policies and only white share-cropper families were permitted to rent-to-own the Plum Bayou farms, there were always black families coming to help manually plant, cultivate, and harvest the crops. Here I began to know blacks, and my mother and father talked with blacks as friends. One of my fondest memories is of Lee Wilson, who

Supporters of Governor Faubus' policy of closing public schools to avoid racial desegregation march up the steps of the Arkansas State Capitol in August 1959.

I have always thought was my father's best friend. Mr. Wilson was a massive black man who made his living carrying railroad ties. He and my father would talk for hours, especially when my father was troubled. As an acknowledgment of the segregation mores, I was taught to call my dad's friend "Lee," not "Mr. Wilson," but I knew that he was a man to whom respect should be shown.

When World War II came, my dad went into military service, and my mother, brother, and I moved to Little Rock. Our neighborhood was racially mixed. While the city had institutional racial segregation, neighborhoods were not nearly so segregated as in many northern cities. There were often clusters of black families living in predominantly white neighborhoods. I grew up in such a lower-middle-class neighborhood, only a few blocks from the family home of Elizabeth Eckford, one of the Little Rock Nine. White and black kids played together on vacant lot playgrounds, and a black neighbor helped me with my first newspaper route. But when it was time to go to school in the fall, we suddenly became segregated. This never seemed right to me. Nor did it seem right to a number of my white neighborhood friends. Two of these friends, Milton and Claudia Davis, became strong civil rights activists when they volunteered to send their children to previously all-black public schools in Memphis.

Among the reporters and photographers covering the crisis at Central High, there was a spectrum of personal views on school integration. On the *Democrat* staff there were those who strongly supported Governor Faubus' segregationist stand, and there were those, like me, who were critical of his intervention into the desegregation process.

But we were united as a staff in trying to gather and report the news as accurately and fairly as possible. Working under editors Gene Harrington, Marcus George, and Bob McCord, I

Only Russia's launching of *Sputnik*, the first craft sent into outer space, competed with the crisis at Central High for press coverage in the fall of 1957. Here the media crowded around Governor Faubus in a press conference at the Arkansas State Capitol.

learned the professionalism of fair, accurate news reporting that was later the foundation of my journalism teaching.

My paper, the afternoon *Arkansas Democrat,* was the number two newspaper in the city and state. The morning *Arkansas Gazette,* which took pride in having been the first newspaper published west of the Mississippi River, had built a solid reputation as one of America's top regional newspapers. It had a larger circulation and a bigger news staff than the *Democrat.*

During the early weeks of the Little Rock crisis, the *Democrat* did an excellent job competing with the *Gazette.* The confrontations at Central High took place early in the morning, and we had time to cover the stories for that afternoon's edition. Later, when the story shifted to the federal courtrooms, the time advantage swung to the *Gazette,* which had the day and night to develop stories for its morning edition.

But the most important difference between the papers was the *Gazette's* editorial stance. Harry Ashmore, editor of the *Gazette,* became the leading, practically the only, critic of Governor Faubus' segregationist policies. For its courageous coverage during the desegregation years, the *Gazette* was applauded by the national press. In 1957 the paper won Pulitzer prizes for Meritorious Service and for Harry Ashmore's editorials.

On the other hand, my paper, the *Democrat,* took an "ostrich" editorial stance during the school-desegregation crisis. Its editorial page editor, Frank Johnson, undoubtedly in consultation with the paper's publisher and owner, August Engle, chose to withhold comment about the city's trauma at Central High. The paper did not even editorially condemn the violence.

One of the *Democrat's* editors recalls an incident that highlighted the frustration of many on the news staff with the paper's weak editorial stance. On the morning of one of the major confrontations at Central High, the editor was standing beside 81-year-old Frank Johnson in the paper's men's room. During casual conversation, he offered the comment, "That was some story out at Central High." Johnson responded, "Yes, it was; I plan to write about it tomorrow." The editor wasn't too surprised when he read the next day's paper. Johnson's editorial was about President Calvin Coolidge, not the desegregation crisis going in Little Rock.

The *Democrat's* lack of editorial backbone paid off in the paper's circulation. The governor and those opposed to desegregation gave their support to the *Democrat* as they called for a boycott of the *Gazette.* Financially the *Gazette* suffered for its strong editorial policy, losing advertising lineage and circulation.

The *Gazette* never recovered from the financial losses. In the 1980s, most American cities were becoming one-newspaper towns. The new owner of the *Democrat* changed to morning delivery, setting off a circulation war with the *Gazette.* In 1986, owner Andrew Heiskel sold the *Gazette* to the Gannett newspaper chain. After five years of intense and expensive competition with the *Democrat,* Gannett chose surrender, and Little Rock's paper became the *Arkansas Democrat Gazette.*

First Day at Central High

Governor Faubus' dramatic act in ordering National Guard troops to Little Rock Central High "to protect the peace" was the fire alarm for Little Rock's news media. Before that, I wasn't even scheduled to go to the school, but suddenly everything changed, and every available news photographer was assigned to the big story.

I carried only a Nikon S2 camera with a wide-angle lens. This 35mm format camera was then rarely used by newspaper photographers, but the small camera gave me a substantial technical advantage over the other photographers, who were shooting with the then-standard 4" x 5" Speed Graphic press cameras. I was able to shoot thirty-six exposures without reloading, while the others had to reload after each shot.

In only my fourth month as a working photojournalist, I was trying to follow my idol, the French photographer Henri Cartier-Bresson. He believed that an event could best be photographed by shooting many exposures with the 35mm camera, working to capture on film the "Decisive Moment," that fraction of a second that would sum up the essence of the event in both content and composition.

At the school on Wednesday, September 4, 1957, the news media didn't know where, or if, the black students would attempt to pass through the Arkansas National Guard troops. The massive school stretches for two blocks, between 14th and 16th along Park Street. For some unknown reason, newsmen started gathering near the 16th Street entrance, and quickly the media pack was clustered there.

As I was standing with this group of newsmen, George Douthit, an *Arkansas Democrat* reporter who covered the governor's office, advised me to go to 14th and Park streets. Douthit had gained the confidence of Governor Faubus and often had advance information about his plans. Some critics, even on the *Democrat* staff, would say that he had too close a personal relationship. I elected to leave the media pack and go to the corner as he had suggested.

There were only a couple of other newsmen waiting at 14th and Park when Elizabeth Eckford approached the National Guardsmen. White students had been passing through the line of troops along the sidewalk. I had suspicions but no real knowledge that the Guardsmen had orders to bar the black students from entering.

Divine guidance may have placed me in the best possible position to see and photograph Elizabeth Eckford as she approached the school. When she was turned away by the National Guard troops, the courage and grace she exhibited as she walked two blocks through the mob of school-integration dissidents became one of my most moving experiences. Her actions epitomized for me the nonviolent principles Dr. Martin Luther King Jr. and the Southern Christian Leadership Conference had begun using to compel the country toward racial justice.

But this 15-year-old girl wasn't part of the national civil rights movement. She has said that she wished to go to Central High school because she wanted to be a lawyer, and she believed that the excellent academic reputation and the wider course offerings at the school would help her toward that career goal. Before she became the first black student to attempt to enter Central High, Elizabeth had not met Daisy Bates, president of the Arkansas National Association for the Advancement of Colored People. She believes she was chosen by the Little Rock School District to be one of the Little Rock Nine because she wasn't tied to the NAACP.

Elizabeth's family was poor and didn't have a telephone in their home. Daisy Bates cites this as her reason for not informing Elizabeth of the plan for all the students to meet at the Bateses' home and go to Central High accompanied by a group of black and white ministers. Instead she came to school as instructed by the school's office, with the understanding that the National Guardsmen were there to protect her as she entered.

Her imperturbable walk through the mob has become a slow-motion *cinema verité* memory. I still find it difficult to believe that this display of racial hatred was happening in front of my high school and my camera.

As I watched and composed the photographs, I didn't know what might happen after each step Elizabeth took. The mob became increasingly strident, and while I saw no one attempt to strike Elizabeth, that possibility was always present. The National Guard troops remained on the sidewalk, passively watching the crowd verbally assail her. It was only as she neared the bus stop at 16th and Park streets that a National Guard officer briefly moved into the crush of demonstrators.

Elizabeth has told me that as she was sitting on a bench at the bus stop, she wondered why the newsmen, including me, who crowded around didn't assist her onto a bus. I have no good answer for her question.

Elizabeth Eckford on Her First Day

Elizabeth says it is still just too painful to go over and over her experience of being taunted by Arkansas National Guardsmen and the segregationist mob as she attempted to become the first black student to enroll at Central High. Instead she looked over the following quotations, which have been attributed to her, and says they are accurate. They have appeared in several publications, including Martin B. Luberman's documentary play *Only in America*. She believes that she originally told her story either to a *New York Herald Tribune* reporter or in a deposition that she gave to the FBI.

"The night before, I was so excited I couldn't sleep. In the morning I was about the first one up. While I was pressing my black and white dress—I had made it to wear on the first day of school—my little brother turned on the TV set. They started telling about a large crowd gathered at the school. The man on TV said he wondered if we were going to show up that morning. Mother called from the kitchen, where

The corner was calm, without any shouting, as Elizabeth approached. The large crowd in front of the school didn't immediately rush to her as she approached the Guardsmen.

she was fixing breakfast, 'Turn that TV off!' She was so upset and worried. I wanted to comfort her, so I said, 'Mother, don't worry.'

"Dad was walking back and forth from room to room with a sad expression. He was chewing on his pipe, and he had a cigar in his hand, but he didn't light either one. It would have been funny, only he was so nervous.

"Before I left home, Mother called us into the living room. She said we should have a word of prayer. Then I caught the bus and got off a block from the school. I saw a large crowd of people standing across the street from the soldiers guarding Central. As I walked on, the crowd suddenly got very quiet. Superintendent Blossom had told us to enter by the front door. I looked at all the people and thought, 'Maybe I will be safer if I walk down the block to the front entrance behind the guards.'

"At the corner I tried to pass through the long line of guards around the school so as to enter the grounds behind them. One of the guards pointed across the street. So I pointed in the same direction—and asked whether he meant for me to cross the street and walk down. He nodded 'yes.' So I walked across the street, then someone shouted, 'Here she comes, get ready!' I moved away from the crowd on the sidewalk and into the street. If a mob came at me, I could then cross back over so the guards could protect me.

"The crowd moved in closer and then began to follow me, calling me names. I still wasn't afraid. Just a little bit nervous. Then my knees began to shake all of a sudden, and I wondered whether I could make it to the center entrance a block away. It was the longest block I ever walked in my whole life.

"Even so, I still wasn't too scared, because all the time I kept thinking that the guards would protect me.

"When I got to the front of the school, I went straight up to a guard again. But this time he just looked straight ahead and didn't move to let me pass him. I didn't know what to do. Then I looked and saw that the path leading to the front entrance was a little further ahead. So I walked until I was right in front of the path to the front door.

"I stood looking at the school—it looked so big! Just then the guards let some white students through.

"The crowd was quiet. I guess they were waiting to see what was going to happen.

"When I was able to steady my knees, I walked up to the guard who had let the white students in. He didn't move. When I tried to squeeze

For me the Little Rock Crisis began as National Guardsmen allowed a white student to pass through their line while Elizabeth Eckford was directed away.

past him, he raised his bayonet, and then the other guards moved in, and they raised their bayonets.

"They glared at me with a mean look, and I was very frightened and didn't know what to do. I turned around, and the crowd came toward me. They moved closer and closer.

"I tried to see a friendly face somewhere in the mob—somebody who maybe would help. I looked into the face of an old woman, but when I looked at her again, she spat on me.

"I turned back to the guards, but their faces told me I wouldn't get any help from them. Then I looked down the block and saw a bench at the bus stop. I thought, 'If I can only get there, I will be safe.' I don't know why the bench seemed a safe place to me, but I started walking toward it. I tried to close my mind to what they were shouting, and kept saying to myself, 'If I can only make it to the bench, I will be safe.'

"When I finally got there, I don't think I could have gone another step. I sat down, and the mob hollered, 'Drag her over to this tree!' Just then a white man sat down beside me, put his arm around me, and patted my shoulder. He raised my chin and said, 'Don't let them see you cry.'

Several other people sat beside Elizabeth at the bus stop, including L. C. Bates, husband of Arkansas NAACP chapter

As the crowd of school integration resisters began falling in behind Elizabeth, many newsmen began following her walk.

Sammie Dean Parker, in black dress, was one of the most fanatical protesters following Elizabeth Eckford. As the crisis developed, she became a self-appointed spokesperson for the student protesters. After Minnijean Brown, one of the black students, was expelled for pouring a bowl of chili on a taunting white student in the school lunchroom, Sammie Dean was also expelled for distributing cards reading "One down, eight to go." Hazel Bryan Massery, the dark-haired girl who walked alongside Sammie Dean and behind Elizabeth, says that her friend Sammie Dean doesn't now wish to talk about her actions in 1957.

Elizabeth had been told that the National Guardsmen were at the school to help her, and in this one instance maybe she *was* aided when an officer walked into the increasingly threatening crowd and seemed to calm it.

president Daisy Bates, and publisher and editor of the *State Press* newspaper. Grace Lorch, who helped Elizabeth to a city bus, and her husband, Lee, a Philander Smith College professor, were accused by Governor Faubus of being communists.

"I can't remember much about the bus ride, but the next thing I remember I was standing in front of the School for the Blind, where Mother works. I ran upstairs, and I kept running until I reached Mother's classroom.

"Mother was standing at the window with her head bowed, but she must have sensed I was there because she turned around. She looked as if she had been crying, and I wanted to tell her I was all right. But I couldn't speak. She put her arms around me, and I cried."

On hearing that other black students had approached the school, I left Elizabeth before she was able to get safely on a city bus and went back to photograph the other students' encounter with the National Guardsmen. In bowtie behind Elizabeth was *New York Times* education reporter Benjamin Fine, who sat with her and advised her not to let them see her cry.

39

As I saw Hazel Bryan's contorted face in the camera's viewfinder, I knew that I had released the shutter at an important moment. At this point my concern was with whether the lens was in focus, with the correct exposure for the uneven light under the trees.

Hazel Bryan Massery

Many have said that if the integration of black and white students at Central High had been left up to the students, without parental or other adult interference, the desegregation process might have worked out without the years of racial tension that have existed outside and inside the school. Now, some of the survivors of those tumultuous years support this viewpoint.

Only a few of the segregation resisters who tried to block the black students' entry in 1957 were of high school age. One of those teenagers, Hazel Bryan, now recalls that she went along with her parents to Central High on the morning that black students were scheduled to enroll to protest the racial integration of the school that she was scheduled to attend.

"I felt very religious at that time. I attended church every Sunday morning and night, as well as Wednesday nights. While no one at church said that we should protest school integration, we got the feeling that it would be a good thing to do," Hazel said.

Because her parents did not want her attending school with the few blacks scheduled to attend Central High, Hazel transferred a few weeks after she was photographed as a central figure taunting Elizabeth. On her first day at Fuller High School, an all-white school near Little Rock, she met Antoine Massery, whom she would marry during her senior year of high school.

A few years later, as her three children were growing up, Hazel's racial attitudes changed, and she realized that her racist actions at Central High were wrong. She says that she knew then that she had done a great injustice to Elizabeth, and she began contemplating what atonement she might make. In 1963, she was able to contact Elizabeth by phone at Elizabeth's father's home and apologize for her actions in the Central High mob. This was a personal conversation between Hazel and Elizabeth and received little media reporting. Hazel doesn't even recall telling her husband or family about this conversation. She says she continued to feel like she was "the poster child for the hate generation, trapped in the image captured in the photograph, and I knew that my life was more than that moment."

Hazel's opportunity to meet and personally make amends to Elizabeth came in 1997, during the days leading up to President Clinton's speech at Central High commemorating the fortieth anniversary of the school's integration. Several reporters, including Michael Leahy of the *Arkansas Democrat Gazette* and Ron Clayburn of ABC News, sought her out for interviews. Arkansas historian Elizabeth Jacoway shared with me her belief that Hazel really wanted to meet Elizabeth and that I might help expedite this meeting.

Elizabeth was one of the speakers at the dedication of the Central High Visitors Center and Museum across the street from the school. After the ceremony, I asked her if she would agree to pose for a photograph with Hazel. Her reply was, "I've wanted to meet her." We made plans

Elizabeth Eckford and Hazel Bryan Massery in front of Little Rock High School in anticipation of President Clinton's speech commemorating the fortieth anniversary of the 1957 desegregation.

for my wife, Vivian, and me to drive Hazel to Elizabeth's home for the meeting.

When they first met, Hazel said, "Elizabeth, thank you so much for agreeing to meet with me." Elizabeth responded, "You are a very brave person to face the cameras again." Soon thereafter the three, Elizabeth, Hazel, and Vivian, were deep in conversation about their flower gardens and what dress Elizabeth might wear for the photograph of the two of them together in front of Central High.

The next day the photograph of the two was published by the *Arkansas Democrat Gazette* and distributed around the world by the Associated Press. Elizabeth and Hazel have since appeared together to sign posters of their Central High reconciliation and on programs at several universities. In late 1998, together they attended a workshop on "racial healing." Elizabeth cautions us not to read too much into this reconciliation photograph; it doesn't mean that all racial issues have been solved in Little Rock. What it *does* mean is that these two women, who had a racial encounter more than forty years ago, have decided to try to put that unpleasant chapter of their lives behind them.

I was delighted several months later when Hazel called to share that she and Elizabeth were going to lunch together just for "girl talk," without any media tagging along.

A few minutes earlier, an officer of the Arkansas National Guard had used his baton to calm the crowd threatening Elizabeth, but here Lt. Col. Marion Johnson uses his baton to block the path of Carlotta Walls and Jefferson Thomas. Johnson said he was acting under orders from Governor Orval Faubus.

The Little Rock Nine

Only minutes after Elizabeth Eckford was refused admittance, the rest of the Little Rock Nine came to Central High accompanied by a group of black and white ministers. They received the same rejection. Actually, the Arkansas National Guardsmen turned away ten black students. One student, Jane Hill, decided to return to all-black Horace Mann High School after facing the hostile crowd that first day.

The young Arkansans who stayed and began desegregation in Little Rock are a remarkable group. They all completed the

As Arkansas National Guardsmen formed a barricade blocking them from Central High on September 4, 1957, black students talked with newsmen before leaving.

A tenth student, Jane Hill (at right), was with the Nine when they attempted to enroll at Central High on September 4th. Hill came to Central only that first day. After she and the other black students were denied entry, she elected to return to Horace Mann and continue her schooling at the all-black high school.

L. C. Bates carved the turkey for the Little Rock Nine at Thanksgiving dinner in his Little Rock home in 1957. From left are Terrence Roberts, Melba Patillo, Thelma Mothershed, L. C. and Daisy Bates, Jefferson Thomas, Elizabeth Eckford, and Ernest Green.

1957–58 school year while studying under near-constant harassment from a hard-core group of white students who were determined to make life miserable for them.

Because of the real possibility of violence in this hostile environment, the black students were each provided a military escort whenever they were at Central High. The only place the male soldiers could not go was into the restrooms with the girls. Melba Patillo Beals has said that she hated to have to use the restroom, because this was where much of the physical harassment occurred.

Because the National Association for the Advancement of Colored People represented the students at their many 1957 federal court appearances, many believe that Daisy Bates, president of the Arkansas NAACP, hand-picked the nine. She certainly did help organize the students after they had been chosen from the more than 150 black students who requested transfers to Central High. But several of the nine have denied that the NAACP selected them. They say they replied to Little Rock School District questionnaires asking if they would like to transfer from their all-black school to the academically superior Central High. Daisy Bates supported the students' version of their selection when she wrote in her book *The Long Shadow of Little Rock* that the Little Rock School Board selected the students on the basis of intelligence, character, health, and maybe even skin color.

Solid academic records were certainly a primary criterion for selection. All nine overcame the disruptions and physical threats, going on to achieve outstanding academic records. The only senior among them, Ernest Green, became assistant secretary of Housing and Urban Affairs in President Carter's administration.

When Governor Faubus, with Little Rock voters' approval, closed the Little Rock public high schools to all students, black

Emogene Wilson posed in 1997 with photographs of her husband being beaten by the Central High mob. In 1957 she was also a journalist, but when her husband was attacked she was on maternity leave, taking care of their four-month-old daughter.

and white, for the 1958–59 school year, most of the Little Rock Nine left Arkansas to continue their schooling. Many never returned to live in Arkansas. When the school-closing bills were ruled unconstitutional in 1959, and the Little Rock high schools reopened and the desegregation process continued, only two of the original Nine, Carlotta Walls and Jefferson Thomas, returned to graduate from Central High. Since then, except for Elizabeth Eckford, they have settled across the country and in Sweden and Canada.

Alex Wilson

Several days after Elizabeth's harrowing walk, the Nine were set to try again to enter the school. Another mob awaited them, but this time the students managed to peacefully enter through a side door. Alex Wilson and a handful of other black journalists unwittingly provided a diversion when they became the target of the mob's rage. Wilson was at the school to report the story for his newspaper, the *Memphis Tri-State Defender.*

Civil rights confrontations were nothing new for Wilson. He had been in Mississippi in 1955 to cover the lynching of Emmett Till, a young black who was killed for allegedly not showing the "proper respect" to a white girl. Wilson was considered the top civil rights reporter for Defender Publications, a national chain of black newspapers.

His stoic response during the attack didn't change as he was knocked to the ground, hit on the head with a brick, and kicked while he was kneeling. As the mob yelled "Run, nigger, run," Wilson continued walking, clutching his hat in his hand and refusing to yield to the racist taunts. He later told his wife, Emogene, "They would have had to kill me before I would have run." He returned to Memphis and his job of editing the newspaper, not talking or complaining about the beating he suffered at Central High. Wilson's wife was home on maternity leave from her job as a reporter, tending to their four-month-old daughter, Karen. She says Wilson didn't talk much to her about the attack, but she noticed his health begin to slip. He was a proud man and refused to see a doctor about the chronic headaches he suffered after the attack.

His work at Central High, and through the South, earned Wilson a promotion to editor of the *Chicago Daily Defender* in 1959. But he continued to experience bad health, and within a few months his rapidly progressing illness was diagnosed as Parkinson's disease. He died in October 1960.

Emogene Wilson returned to Memphis to teach school and raise their child near her family. Mrs. Wilson believes the legacy her husband left has been an inspiration to their daughter, Dr. Karen Rose Wilson-Sadberry, who was a professor at Texas A&M University for eight years before leaving in 1996 for the birth of her son, Adam.

Shortly after he was attacked, Mr. Wilson recounted for his newspapers and the *New York Journal-American* his beating by the mob:

"I was one of the three Negro newsmen and a freelance photographer who were attacked by a shabby, hate-filled mob of segregationists Monday near Central High School, at 16th and Park.

"The others assaulted were James Hicks, managing editor of the Amsterdam News; *Moses J. Newsom, of the Afro-American newspapers; and Earl Davy, freelance photographer of Little Rock.*

"I did not leave my post as general manager and editor of the Memphis Tri-State Defender, *a member of the Defender Publications, with any desire or intention of projecting myself into the national limelight.*

"I knew before I came to Little Rock that the assignment would be a tough one. The task had to be performed, and only a veteran should take it. Common sense dictated that I perform the duty.

"Any newsman worth his salt is dedicated to the proposition that it is his responsibility

An angry mob surrounded Mr. Wilson as he did not heed their taunts to "Run, nigger, run!" The mob had attacked and chased away three other black journalists who accompanied Wilson on September 23, 1957. But Alex Wilson would not run, even when it became clear that the police would not intervene.

to report the news under favorable and unfavorable conditions. I strive to serve in the category.

"It was my hope, and others in the group with me, that regardless of our color, we would be permitted to perform our duties like others of paler hue.

"But lo, in this great land of the free, and home of the brave, we felt the deep-seated hatred of an element who can only understand the fist of the law, which was not evident in our case.

"The disgraceful incident (especially in a city which professes to be progressive) occurred about 8:20 A.M. Monday, near the 16th and Park Street entrance of Central High.

"I parked my car about two blocks from the intersection. Newsom and I were in front, with Hicks and Davy following, when we began the long, apprehensive walk.

"We had firsthand knowledge of where the nine stout-hearted Negro students were to enter, and we set off at a fast clip to be on hand when they arrived at the campus entrance.

"About midway of the final block, we picked up a tail of two whites. They made no comment. We kept moving forward.

"A crowd of about one hundred faced the school (away from us), waiting for the nine students to appear.

"Then, someone in the crowd of whites spotted us advancing.

"Suddenly the angry eyes of the entire pack were upon us. We moved forward to within ten feet of the mob. Two men spread their arms in eagle fashion. One shouted: 'You'll not pass!'

"I said: 'We are newspapermen.' Hicks added, 'We only want to do our job.'

"'You'll not pass!' one of the pack yelled back.

"I tried to move to the left of the mob, but my efforts were thwarted. I made a half-turn left from the sidewalk and went over to a Little Rock policeman, who was standing mid-center of the street.

"'What is your business?' he asked. I presented my press card. He took his time checking it. Then he said: 'You better leave. Go on across to the sidewalk' (away from the mob at my heels).

Mr. Wilson and his assailants were quickly moving past me, and I kept shooting even though I realized that the movement was probably too fast to freeze with the slow film (80 ISO) in my camera.

"I followed his suggestion. After taking several steps, I looked back. The officer was near the opposite sidewalk, leaving the angry pack to track me.

"The mob struck. I saw Davy being roughed up. Hicks and Newsom were retreating from kicks and blows. I stopped momentarily, as the hoots and jeers behind me increased.

"Strangely, the vision of Elizabeth Eckford, one of the nine students, flashed before me as she with dignity strode through a jeering, hooting gauntlet of segregationists several days ago.

"Maybe, too, my training as a U.S. Marine in World War II and my experience as a war correspondent in Korea, and work on the Emmett Till case influenced my decision during that moment of crisis.

"I decided not to run. If I were to be beaten, I'd take it walking if I could—not running.

I was startled to see that an old school classmate and friend, Joe Elder (on the left, in the dark coat), was one of the mob.

Joe Elder

As Mr. Wilson was being beaten, I recognized in the mob an old classmate, Joe Elder. Joe had been my classmate, first at Robert E. Lee Elementary, then at West Side Junior High and Little Rock High School. (The school was renamed Central High in 1956, after Hall High School was completed on Little Rock's affluent northwest side the year before integration was to begin at Central.)

When I saw him in the crowd, I recall asking, "Joe, what the hell are you doing here?" Forty years later, Joe recalled speaking to me that day but doesn't recall my question. He does now recall, "I learned that morning how easy it is to get caught up in the emotions and actions of a mob."

Joe says that when the verbal abuse of Alex Wilson turned to violence, "I realized that it was wrong and I retreated." (My sequence of photographs does seem to show Joe moving away from Mr. Wilson after the physical violence began.)

Two days after the attack on Mr. Wilson, Joe says he called Daisy Bates, president of the Arkansas NAACP, to apologize for his presence in the mob. She asked for his name, but Joe says he refused to give it to her because of fear of police reprisals. In an incident that was probably unrelated, a couple of days later he was questioned by the FBI but not arrested.

"On that Monday morning I was going to visit my parents, who lived a couple blocks south of Central High on Park Street. My mother had been released from the hospital a few days earlier and I wanted to visit her. The Little Rock city policemen refused to allow me to pass through their lines, and I had to detour several blocks around the school. When I told my dad of the policemen not letting me through, he said, "They can't do that. Let's go up there." So we went to see what was going on. We didn't do anything after we got there; in fact, I think he went across into a vacant lot where there was a small terrace." Joe said that he could not identify his dad in any of my photographs.

"When the crowd started following Wilson, after Wilson had been told to leave by a Little Rock policeman, I joined them. I followed him for only a short distance, until I heard that they were looking for a rope to hang that man. I thought 'This is no place for me to be,' and I turned and walked back to 16th and Park. This is when Gene Smith (assistant chief of the Little Rock Police Department), who had lived in our neighborhood when we were growing up, came up to me and began swearing and asking me what I was doing there. I began swearing back at him, and the police were getting ready to take me to jail, until Smith found out his conversation with me was being taped by a reporter. Then Smith said to me, 'Get out, leave.' I left and didn't return to the school anytime during the crisis."

After a medical disability forced Joe to retire as a sign painter in 1980, he moved to Mississippi with his wife, Marta, to be near the VA Medical Center in Biloxi. There he has taken up a part-time career as a portrait painter. His work has appeared in several Mississippi art galleries, and he has painted such personalities as U.S. Senator Trent Lott.

"I now believe that it is OK for white and black kids to go to a nearby school together. But I don't feel that it is right to force them to go to school together. In fact, I don't believe in 'forced' anything." Because of poor health, Joe hasn't visited his Little Rock home for many years. Recently I asked him if he would like to talk with Alex Wilson's widow, Emogene. He responded, "I don't know *what* I could say to her."

Joe Elder in his Mississippi art studio

I have never been so nervous as I was during the minutes it took to process this roll of film. I recalled that most of Robert Capa's film of the World War II D-Day invasion was destroyed in processing. So I was elated to see that there were images, and this one (*opposite page*) showed me, early in my photojournalism career, that most often the best photographs are easily chosen. Its composition just leaped out from the others. It was reasonably sharp with good exposure. In the 1960s it was selected by the National Press Photographers Association and the University of Missouri as one of the fifty outstanding news photographs of the century.

"Members of the red-blooded democracy-loving mob acted swiftly. They sensed (I realize now) my determination.

"One hillbilly kicked at my left side. I broke the impact, not striking back.

"Another unleashed a looping right to my side. It grazed my jaw as I ducked.

"A brave Arkansas 'peckerwood' leaped upon my back, encircling my neck with his arm.

"Thanks to the Marine Corps training, I was able to shake him, without sustaining injury. He backed away with a half-brick (with at least fifty persons behind him), yelling: 'Run, damn you, run!'

"I looked at him and at the brick, then picked up my hat, recreased it, and started walking again.

"A courageous white member of the mob at my back struck me on the back of my head. It was a hefty blow. To keep from falling, I lunged forward from the impact, to regain balance.

"I came upright near an auto, and looked into the tear-filled eyes of a White woman. Although there was sorrow in her eyes, I knew there would not be any help.

"I walked away, and the runt with the half-brick threatened again. (How I wished at the moment we could meet man to man.)

"Someone yelled: 'Don't kill him.'

54

"It was repeated by another in the mob as I staggered toward my car. Someone gave me a push from the rear, adding to the impetus of my retreat.

"Suddenly, I was free of the pack. One man yelled, 'We'll teach you northern niggers about coming down here!'

"What the bigoted creature didn't know is that I am one of many southern-born citizens dedicated to the cause of helping to bring full democracy to this great country of ours.

"Yes, I was abused—a victim of misguided violence—but I am not bitter. If my effort to help bring human dignity in its fullest sense to the oppressed minority here is successful, then the welfare of all will be enhanced."

Back to Central High

THE "LITTLE ROCK CRISIS" photographs have been the bedrock of my career in photojournalism. Primarily on the basis of these images, the Associated Press lured me from Little Rock to Chicago to be an editor and photographer, and my professional experience was an important factor when I was asked to join the Indiana University journalism faculty.

During my thirty-two years of teaching, I used these photographs in just about every class. I always cited them as evidence of the power of the image to communicate the news. I have always believed that good news reporting (both pictures *and* words) did make a difference in Little Rock. And just as my high school teacher did for me, one of my major teaching goals was to help my students understand that responsible news reporting is important for making the world a better place.

Professors learn to sense when their message is getting through to their students. Mine were always interested in my Central High work, and a number have told me that these images inspired them toward journalism careers.

I'd like to say that these photographs and my message were always very well received, but in the early 1990s, as I was showing the desegregation crisis images, a student rose to question my statement that the school was, after once being a landmark of resistance to integration, now a successfully integrated school. She said that she was a graduate of Central's rival, Hall High School, and that Central High had been ruined by integration.

"Do you really know what is going on at Central High School?" she challenged. She then told me stories of gangs and drug dealers and racial confrontations at the school. It left me confused. The story was quite different from what I had heard over the years, but I recall thinking, "What if she's right?"

My teaching philosophy had been built on my appreciation and love of photojournalism and my belief that the Fourth Estate, a responsible press, serves as a balance between the executive, legislative, and judiciary branches of government. Some traditionalists have considered "the press" nearly exclusively the written word, but the reporting at Central High showed that images played a major part in telling the story of racial injustice. President Eisenhower's dispatching of federal

Because of a bomb threat, white students left school early this day in September 1957.

In 1957 it was easy to photograph large numbers of white students in front of Central High, as the school was often emptied because of bomb threats. In the spring of 1997, I mentioned to Principal Rudolph Howard that it didn't appear that I was going to be able to shoot a parallel photograph of the desegregated student body. He came to my rescue with an offer to give me advance notice of the time of a fire drill.

Football but No School

After Governor Faubus announced that he was closing the school to stop racial desegregation, Gene Hall, coach of the Central High Tigers, thought that the football team would not have a 1958 season.

But some parents of football players appealed to the governor not to deprive their sons of the opportunity to play on a championship team. The governor agreed to their request, and the Tigers played a full schedule in 1958. However, their unbeaten streak of forty-three games was stopped when they were beaten by a Baton Rouge, Louisiana, team in the second game of the year.

Before the school was closed, Coach Hall, in his first year as head coach, had 130 players out

In 1999 Gene Hall returned to Central High's Quigley Field, where he was head coach of the Tigers for twelve years.

trying to make the team. After students were barred from attending classes at Central High, the football squad dwindled to 32 players. Coach Hall believes that some of his players attended classes at one of the private high schools established after the governor closed all of Little Rock's public high schools. But Hall says that some of his players attended no classes that fall.

With no students at the school, attendance was way down for the 1958 games. Some of the meager fan support came from federalized National Guard troops who were stationed at Central throughout the year. The troops formed a cheer section at the home games. And even though Central High's teachers had no students to teach, they were under contract to be at school. Coach Hall says that before one game, several teachers dressed in cheerleaders' costumes and led the troops in a pep rally.

During the football season, Coach Hall was "called up" by the Arkansas National Guard to serve with the federalized troops on duty at Central High. Each day his officers let him leave for football practices and games.

With the high school, empty of students, looming in the background, Assistant Coach Allen Howard leads practice for the 1958 Little Rock Central High Tigers.

Billy Watson held the attention of his trigonometry students better than any teacher I have ever seen. Even students who said they didn't like math said that Watson, one of a core of excellent teachers at Central High, made trig an interesting subject.

Martha Brantley and Ryan Davis seemed to be banging their fists together as if they were fighting. After I took their picture, they explained that they were simply demonstrating how to shake hands with closed fists. Ryan was an honor student and Martha class valedictorian of the 1997 class.

troops after seeing my images of the Wilson beating gave me confirmation that good photojournalism can, and does, make a difference.

Good, fair reporting with a camera is an important, indeed essential, tool of good contemporary journalism. Indiana's school of journalism was one of the first to require that all majors have a course in visual journalism. I am pleased that thousands of my students, many of whom have gone on to careers as editors and reporters, left Indiana with a serious exposure to the place of the visual image in journalism.

But what if my young heckler was right about Central High? I had not been back to the school in many years and didn't know how to answer her. My assertion that racial integration was going smoothly was based primarily on scattered news reports and what I heard from friends in Arkansas. She had been a graduate of Central's arch rival, Hall High School, but her taunts continued to trouble me.

After retiring from IU in 1995, I accepted a visiting professorship to teach a semester at my undergraduate alma mater, the University of Central Arkansas in Conway, northwest of Little Rock. My daughter, Claudia, now a picture editor for the Associated Press in New York, suggested that I go back to Central High and document the changes that had occurred since the school was racially desegregated. After all,

Annice Steadman shows the structure of a crab to students in her advanced biology class. Several years ago, Steadman was lured from Central High to build the biology program at the Arkansas magnet school for science and mathematics at Hot Springs. After that program was up and running, she returned to teach in her basement laboratory classroom at Central.

Playing in the band may be one of high school's more enjoyable experiences. These trumpet players, Lee Burdell (left) and Benjamin Alexander, were working hard at a Little Rock Central High Tiger band practice.

the city of Little Rock was planning a commemoration of the fortieth anniversary of the Central High crisis. And while I was delighted to have this opportunity to return to Central in 1997, I was apprehensive about what I might find and photograph.

As I entered the school for the first time in forty years, I expected security to be very tight and that I would need to be escorted everywhere I was allowed to photograph. Over the years, I have photographed inside a number of industrial plants, shopping centers, and some schools, and always I have been escorted. When shooting in a Gary, Indiana, steel plant, I recall that I always had to have three company employees with me. It was different at Central High. After explaining the

purpose of my project to the Little Rock schools superintendent's office and gaining approval, I was introduced to the security personnel by Central's principal, Rudolph Howard. The security staff of ten quietly monitors the comings and goings around the building with the assistance of closed-circuit television monitors and radios carried by each security guard. Principal Howard seems to know what is going on at all times. Soon I felt comfortable working accompanied only by my wife, Vivian.

The majestic structure has aged well. It looks remarkably similar to what I remember from forty years ago. I understand that the school is seeking funding to make needed renovations,

Friends cornrowed Michael Brown's hair in the bleachers during a
1997 basketball game.

Waiting for cheerleading tryouts

Phyllis Caruth, a Central High alumna, counsels with a group of her statistics students working on a semester project. Caruth, the school's second minority National Merit Scholar, returned to Central to teach after graduating from Swarthmore College.

Neither race nor gender appears to be a major factor in the election of student leaders at Central High. Student Council presidents Megan Kearney (left; 1996–97) and Fatima McKendra (1997–98) were photographed as they prepared required forms showing the racial makeup of the Student Council. Between 1994 and 1997, the school had one white male, one black male, one white female, and one black female as Student Council president.

Class President Will Trice danced with Anita Bunche and many of his other classmates at the 1997 Senior Prom.

Desegregation of social activities, such as senior proms, has been difficult in the South, even as the classrooms have become more and more integrated. In 1997, though, all manner of students at Central High celebrated their high school experience.

In their finery, couple Michael Brown (left) and Sherril Shantz Lindsey wait for their turn to parade in the Central High Senior Prom Grand March in 1997.

but the school doesn't appear to be deteriorating. I saw no graffiti at Central High, only posters promoting school election candidates and athletic rivalries.

While the building hasn't changed much since the 1957 crisis, there has been a dramatic transformation toward the desegregation of the school. Now there is a strong commitment from state and city governments and civic and education leaders to make desegregation work.

While in 1957 Governor Orval Faubus blocked desegregation, in 1997 Governor Mike Huckabee, a conservative Republican, speaking at the opening of the Little Rock Central High

Visitors Center, said, "I am not here to block doors to anyone; I am here to open them to everyone." This was dramatically portrayed as he joined President Clinton in opening the doors as the Little Rock Nine returned for the fortieth-anniversay commemoration ceremony.

This attitude is seen all around Little Rock. Now many of the civic leaders not only support Central High with their words, they send their children from affluent suburban neighborhoods to study at Central. In 1998, Huckabee's daughter Sarah became a Central High student.

Of course there are still many problems to overcome.

Principal Rudolph Howard, cleaning the sign before graduation and then presenting diplomas to 1997 graduates in Little Rock's Barton Coliseum.

Graduation day, 1997.

Critics, both black and white, point out that few black students have enrolled in Central's highly acclaimed advanced-placement academic classes. Of the twenty-three National Merit Scholarship semifinalists, only five have been minority students. This racial imbalance concerns the administrators and teachers. They would like more black honor students, but they point out that all students are welcome and are encouraged to enroll in the advanced classes.

On one level my student was right: There *are* gangs and drugs at Central High, and there have been a few racial confrontations as well. But the gangs certainly aren't running the school, and these problems are minimal when compared with the progress toward desegregation that has been made since the 1957 crisis at Central High.

All in all, I found great hope for the future of public schools inside this magnificent building. Central High has always had a reputation as one of the best (if not *the* best) high schools in the state. With African-American students now a majority of the student body, the school's academic reputation only continues to grow.

The school's excellent faculty must be the foundation for creating classes where more than 60 percent of all graduates go on to study at four-year institutions of higher education. And many of the teachers have chosen to remain at this urban inner-city school rather than move to private schools and suburban public schools.

In this time, when some black leaders are suggesting that blacks would be better served with well-funded separate black schools, the administration, faculty, and students of Central High seem committed to making racial integration work and work well. Central's teaching staff should receive much of the credit for the progress. School librarian Elaine Dumas says the faculty sees it as their mission to make desegregation work.

Teaching at Central is considered a choice teaching assignment.

They know that this task is not easy. They also know that Central, because the spotlight of the civil rights movement continues to be pointed its way, has to be more than a "normal" school. Any conflicts, racial or otherwise, will be magnified because it is Little Rock Central High School. Teachers and administrators feel that they live in a fishbowl, but they are very proud of their school.

Fortieth-Anniversary Commemoration

Several times since 1957, the Little Rock Nine have gathered for reunions of their special high school group. While they are now scattered around the world, their experiences at Central High created a lasting bond.

In 1997, with the Little Rock Central High Visitors Center being completed in the old Magnolia gas station across Park Street, and with a native Arkansan, Bill Clinton, serving his second term as president, the fortieth reunion on September 25th became a very special event.

Speaking from the high school steps, President Clinton told the audience of 7,500 that

> a single image of a black student, Elizabeth Eckford, being taunted by whites first seared the heart and stirred the conscience of our nation. Elizabeth Eckford, along with her eight classmates, was turned back on September 4th, but the Little Rock Nine did not turn back. Forty years ago today, they climbed these steps, passed through this door, and moved our nation.

Not everyone was in favor of the commemoration. Some Arkansans suggested that commemorating the state's racist past would merely open old wounds that would be better left untouched. Even the state and local chapters of the NAACP

The lawn, which stretches two city blocks in front of Central High, was crowded with spectators to hear President Clinton speak at the commemoration of the fortieth anniversary of the beginning of desegregation.

Governor Orval Faubus blocked the Little Rock Nine from entering Central High in 1957. In 1997, President Bill Clinton symbolically welcomed them at the front door.

voiced concern that the events would signify that everything is fine in Little Rock.

But now, most of Little Rock's civic leaders support efforts to make Central High a living memorial in the struggle for racial harmony. State and city government agencies have helped fund the $550,000 Visitors Center. Elizabeth Eckford was named to the Board of Directors. Several of those first black students to attend Central say that the images and sounds the museum presents still bring back bad memories of their 1957 experience, but they all express joy that their milestone contribution is being memorialized and appreciated in Little Rock. In 1998, Congress made Central High a National Historical Site. It is the only operating high school with this honor.

Little Rock is still learning to live with the black eye cast by the racism and school closings of the crisis years. Many around town still think the city should move on and not continue to bring attention to those dark years. Other leaders—and they seem to be the majority—believe that the heroic struggle to get the desegregation movement under way will always be an important part of the city's history and must be studied and commended.

Most of the major players—the Little Rock Nine, Governor Orval Faubus, the NAACP, and members of the press—have prospered from their involvement in the Little Rock Central High story. But what about those thousands of students, black and white, who were denied a year of their high school education in 1958–59? Who knows what effect this disruption, and for many of the students the end of their schooling, has had? This group now feels left out of the story.

Civic leaders in Little Rock now believe that the success or failure of desegregation at Central High may well determine the future of public school education in the city and state. Since the crisis of 1957, many private high schools have opened and closed in Little Rock. None of these exclusive schools have approached the academic excellence and course offerings of Central High.

Just how well is desegregation at Central progressing? If one just took a look around the school lunch tables, it wouldn't appear that much social desegregation is taking place. For the most part, white students still gather with other whites, and black students gather with other blacks. But Jenny Holt, a white 1997 graduate, believes that true desegregation is progressing. She says that during her three years at Central she saw

Lauren Perkins is escorted by fellow eleventh-graders Bruce Evans (left) and Tarvoris Uzoigwe as she is introduced as a candidate for Central High's 1999 basketball Homecoming court.

With the opening of the Museum and Visitors Center across from Central High, Elizabeth Eckford and Hazel Massery signed posters showing their clash in 1957 and their reconciliation in 1997. Elizabeth's close friend Annie Abrams stood behind the two. Mrs. Abrams, a Little Rock community leader and a member of the museum's board of directors, has worked hard over the years to improve race relations in Little Rock and to honor the black students who worked for the desegregation of education. In 1997, Elizabeth joined Annie on the board of the museum.

three groups of students: a white group who just wished to "hang out" with other whites, a black group who just wished to "hang out" with other blacks, and a third group who wished to have friends of both races. Reflecting back, she perceived that the number of black and white friendships increased each year.

"The federal government cannot legislate how people feel" was a rallying cry of the segregationists. That is just as true today as it was in 1957, but that fact is *still* irrelevant to how our legal system should operate. And feelings, even the most deeply rooted hatred, can change. The start of desegregation in Little Rock was certainly a violent and searing moment, but the life of Central High since that time has proved again that even our national life is more than any one moment.

The Little Rock Nine returned to Central High forty years after they became the first black students to attend the school. From the left are Melba Patillo Beals, Elizabeth Eckford, Ernest Green, Gloria Ray Karl-mark, Carlotta Walls LaNier, Terrence Roberts, Jefferson A. Thomas, Minnijean Brown Trickey, and Thelma Jean Mothershed Wair.

Little Rock Nine Gold Medals

H.R.2560
LITTLE ROCK NINE MEDALS AND COINS ACT
(Engrossed in House)

Sec. 101. Congressional Findings.

The Congress hereby finds the following.

(1) Jean Brown Trickey, Carlotta Walls LaNier, Melba Patillo Beals, Terrence Roberts, Gloria Ray Karlmark, Thelma Mothershed Wair, Ernest Green, Elizabeth Eckford, and Jefferson Thomas, hereafter in this section referred to as the 'Little Rock Nine', voluntarily subjected themselves to the bitter stinging pains of racial bigotry.

(2) The Little Rock Nine are civil rights pioneers whose selfless acts considerably advanced the civil rights debate in this country.

(3) The Little Rock Nine risked their lives to integrate Central High School in Little Rock, Arkansas, and subsequently the Nation.

(4) The Little Rock Nine sacrificed their innocence to protect the American principle that we are all 'one nation, under God, indivisible'.

(5) The Little Rock Nine have indelibly left their mark on the history of this Nation.

(6) The Little Rock Nine have continued to work towards equality for all Americans.

Sec. 102. Congressional Gold Medals.

(a) PRESENTATION AUTHORIZED—The President is authorized to present, on behalf of the Congress, to Jean Brown Trickey, Carlotta Walls LaNier, Melba Patillo Beals, Terrence Roberts, Gloria Ray Karlmark, Thelma Mothershed Wair, Ernest Green, Elizabeth Eckford, and Jefferson Thomas, commonly referred to collectively as the 'Little Rock Nine', gold medals of appropriate design, in recognition of the selfless heroism such individuals exhibited and the pain they suffered in the cause of civil rights by integrating Central High School in Little Rock, Arkansas.

(b) DESIGN AND STRIKING—For purposes of the presentation referred to in subsection (a), the Secretary of the Treasury shall strike a gold medal with suitable emblems, devices, and inscriptions to he determined by the Secretary for each recipient.

Photograph by Scott Goldsmith

Will Counts decided to make photojournalism his career while studying in Miss Edna Middlebrook's journalism class at Little Rock High School (now Little Rock Central High). During the Central High desegregation crisis between 1957 and 1960, he worked as a photographer for the *Arkansas Democrat,* where his photographs were runner-up for the 1957 Pulitzer Prize in photography. He became a photo editor for the Associated Press in Chicago in 1960, and later an AP photographer in Indianapolis. He is Professor Emeritus of the Indiana University School of Journalism, where he directed the School's photojournalism sequence from 1963 to 1995. In 1997, while a Visiting Professor at his undergraduate alma mater, the University of Central Arkansas, Counts returned to Central High to document the school forty years after the integration crisis. He and his wife, Vivian, also a native Arkansan, live in Bloomington, Indiana.

Will Davis Cambell, author of *Brother to a Dragonfly,* was born in southern Mississippi in 1924. Ordained a Baptist preacher at 17, he briefly attended Louisiana College, then served as a medic in the South Pacific during World War II. After the war he married Brenda Fisher, attended Tulane University, and graduated from Wake Forest University and Yale Divinity School. First as a university chaplain at Ole Miss, then as race relations troubleshooter for the National Council of Churches, and finally as director of an activist organization called the Committee of Southern Churchmen, Campbell was among the most conspicuous of white Southerners for social justice in the civil rights movement of the 1950s and '60s. The author of many books, he has also been the subject of two biographies and numerous profiles in such magazines as *Rolling Stone, Life, The Progressive,* and *Esquire.* Will and Brenda Campbell live on a farm near Mt. Juliet, Tennessee.

Ernest Dumas is a native Arkansan who has spent his entire life in the state except for short sojourns at the University of Missouri and in the U.S. Army. He was reared in the piney woods of South Arkansas, then a citadel of segregation and home to the white citizens' councils. He spent thirty-one years at the *Arkansas Gazette,* one of the nation's great newspapers until its demise in 1991, half that time as a State Capitol and political reporter and later as associate editor and editorial writer. He continues to write a column for the *Arkansas Times* and several other Arkansas newspapers and teaches journalism at the University of Central Arkansas at Conway. In 1992 he edited a book, *The Clintons of Arkansas.*

Robert S. McCord, a native of Arkansas, has spent fifty years working on Arkansas newspapers. At the time of the crisis at Central High School, he was the Sunday Magazine editor of the *Arkansas Democrat* and Will Counts' boss. Later he became editor and publisher of the *North Little Rock Times.* He returned to the *Arkansas Democrat* as executive editor and retired in 1991 as columnist and senior editor of the *Arkansas Gazette.* McCord is a graduate of the University of Arkansas and the Columbia University Graduate School of Journalism.